Animals Coloring Book

For Pre-schoolers, Toddlers

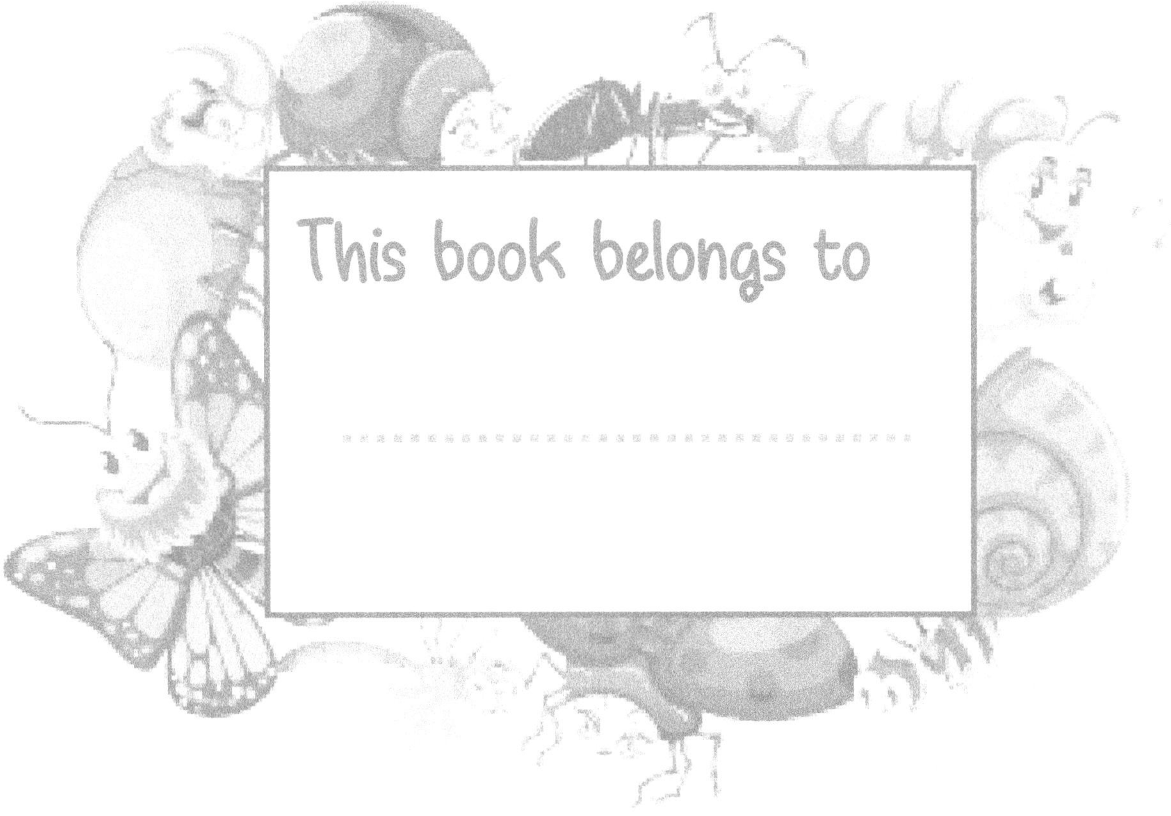

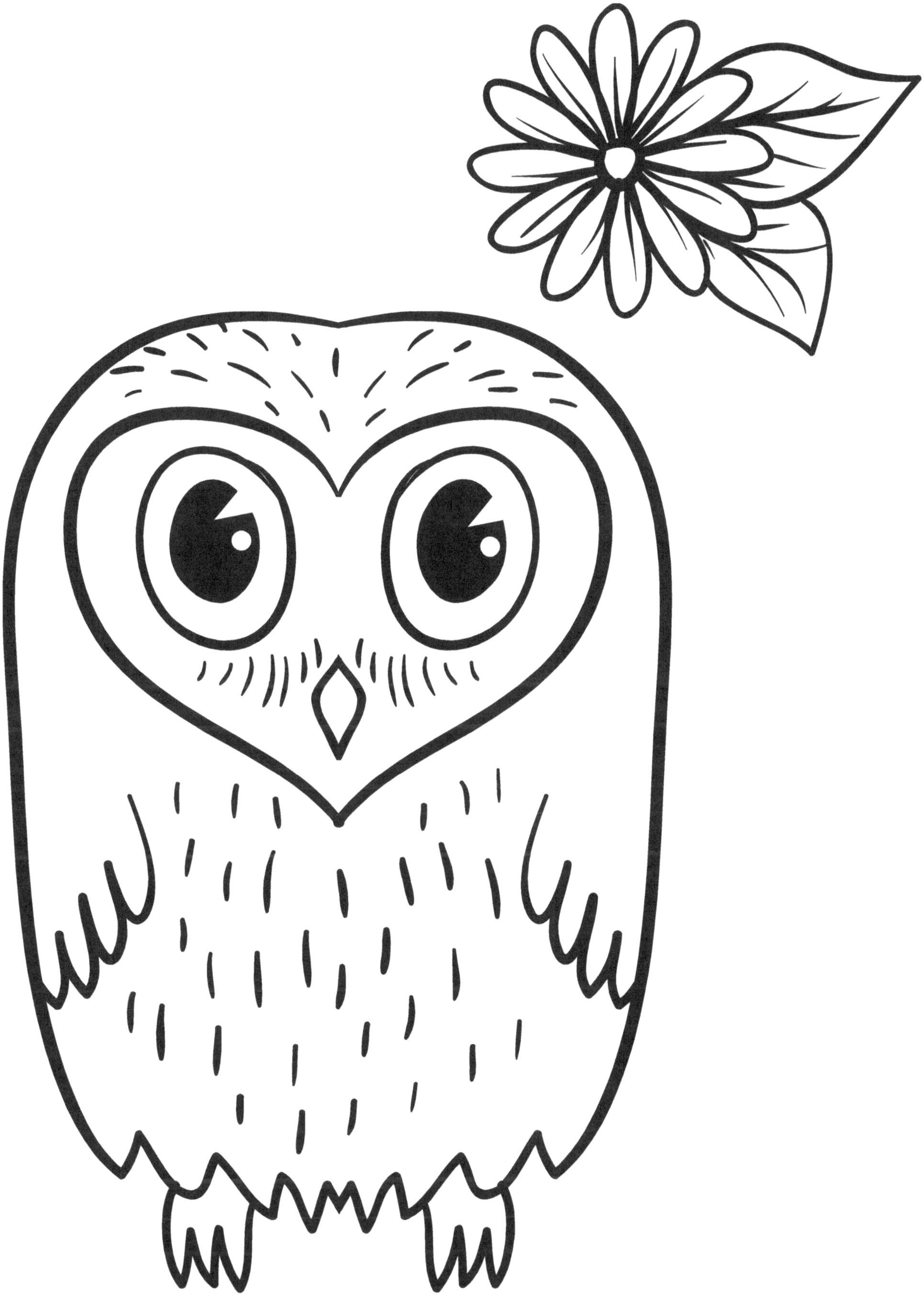

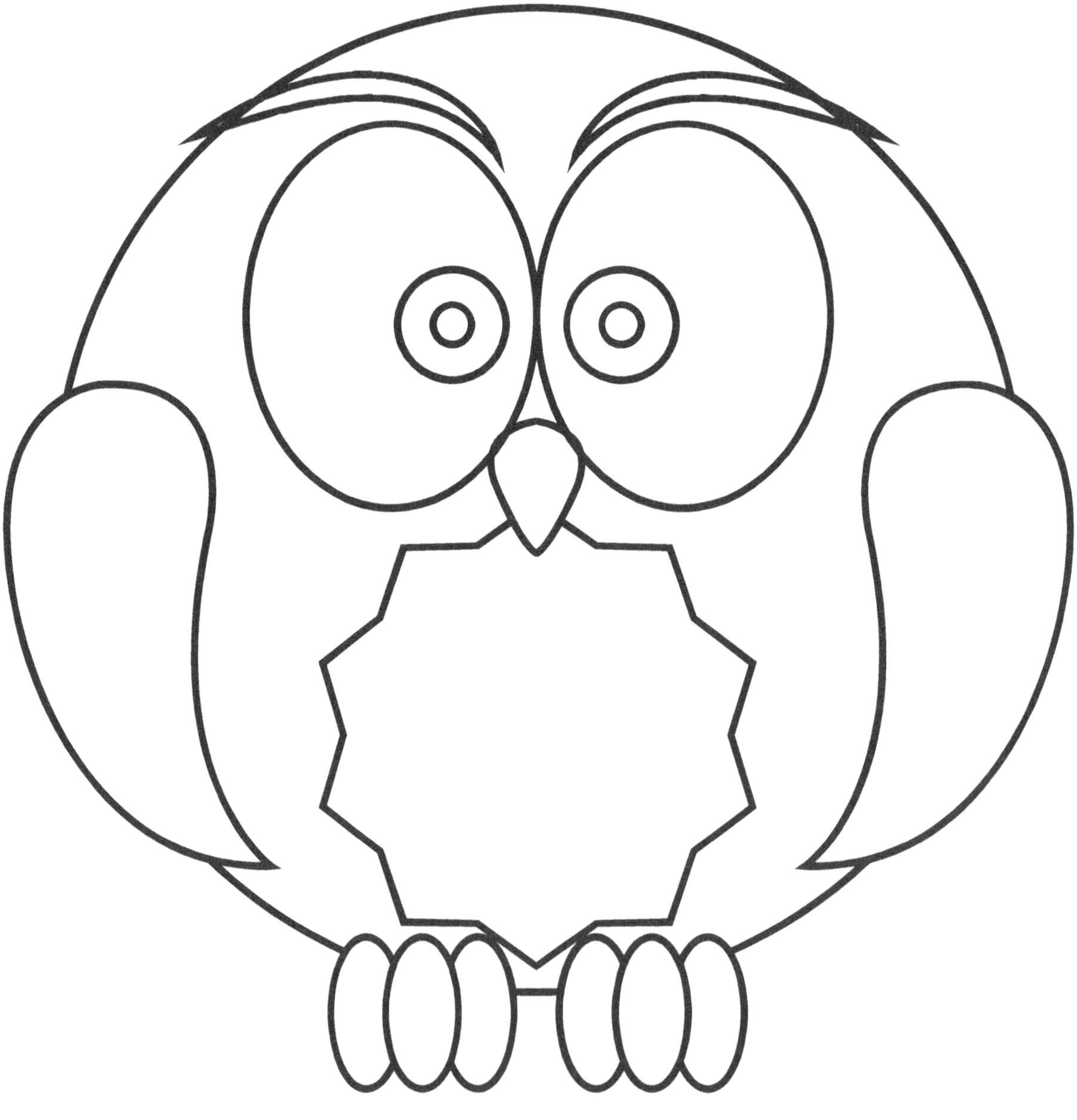

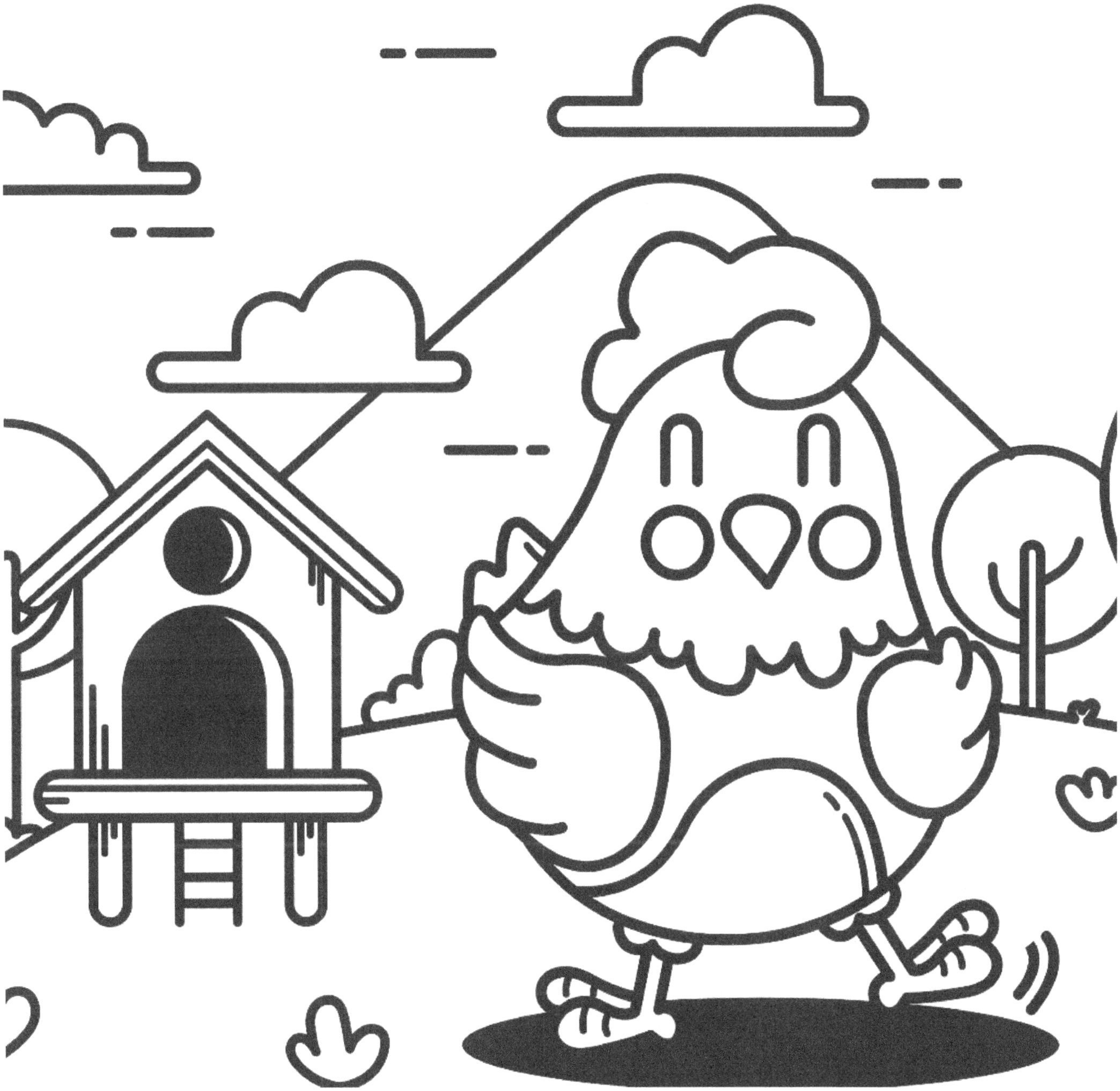

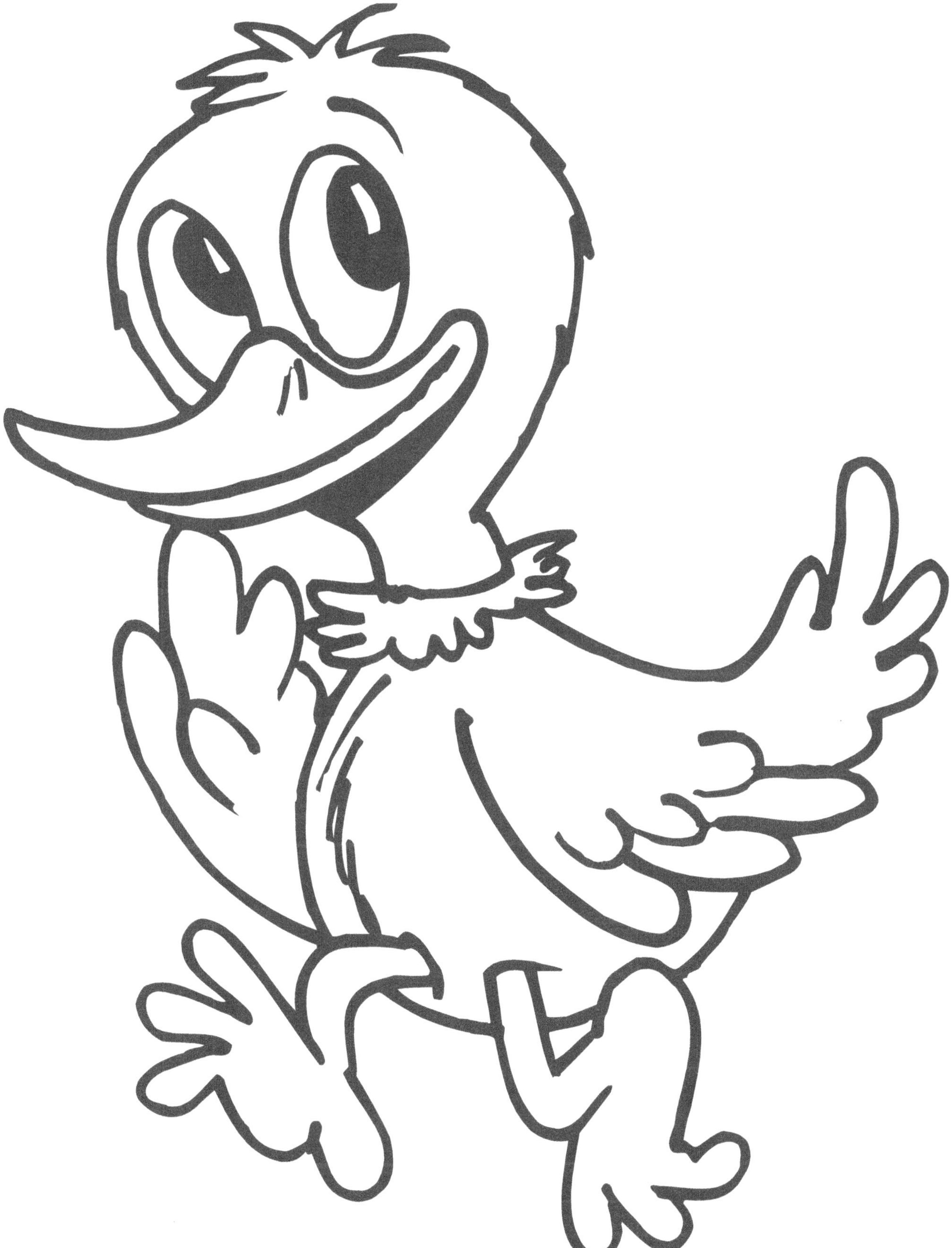

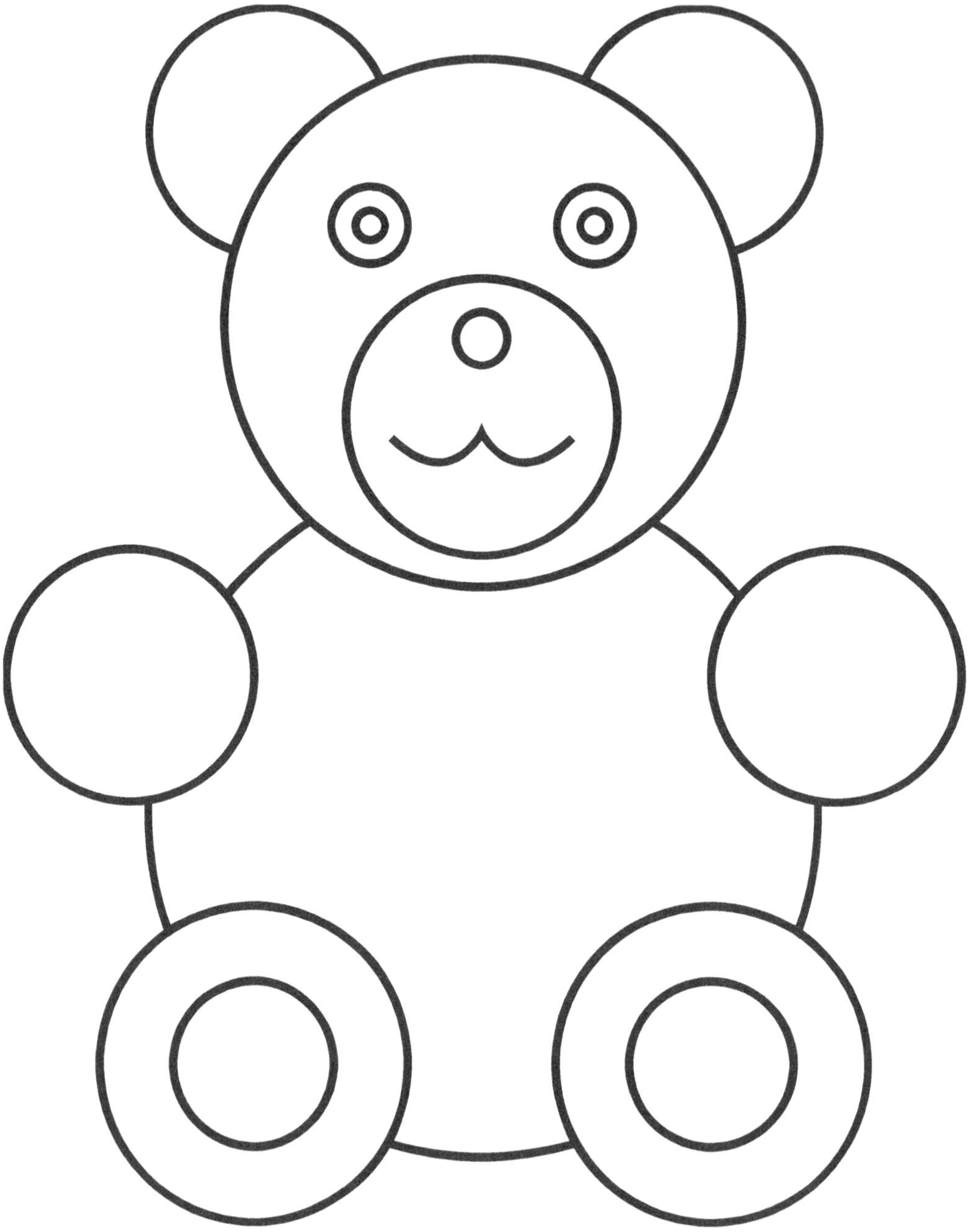

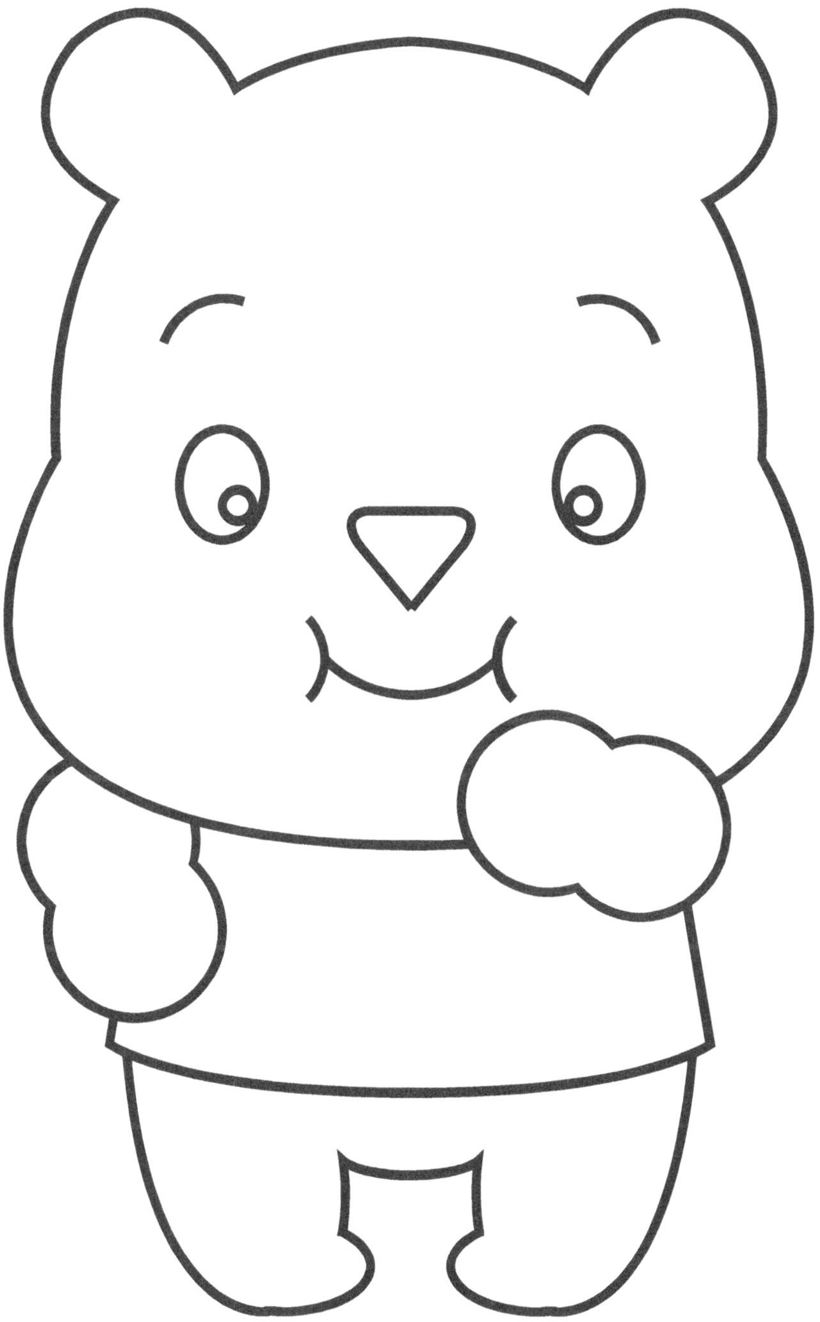

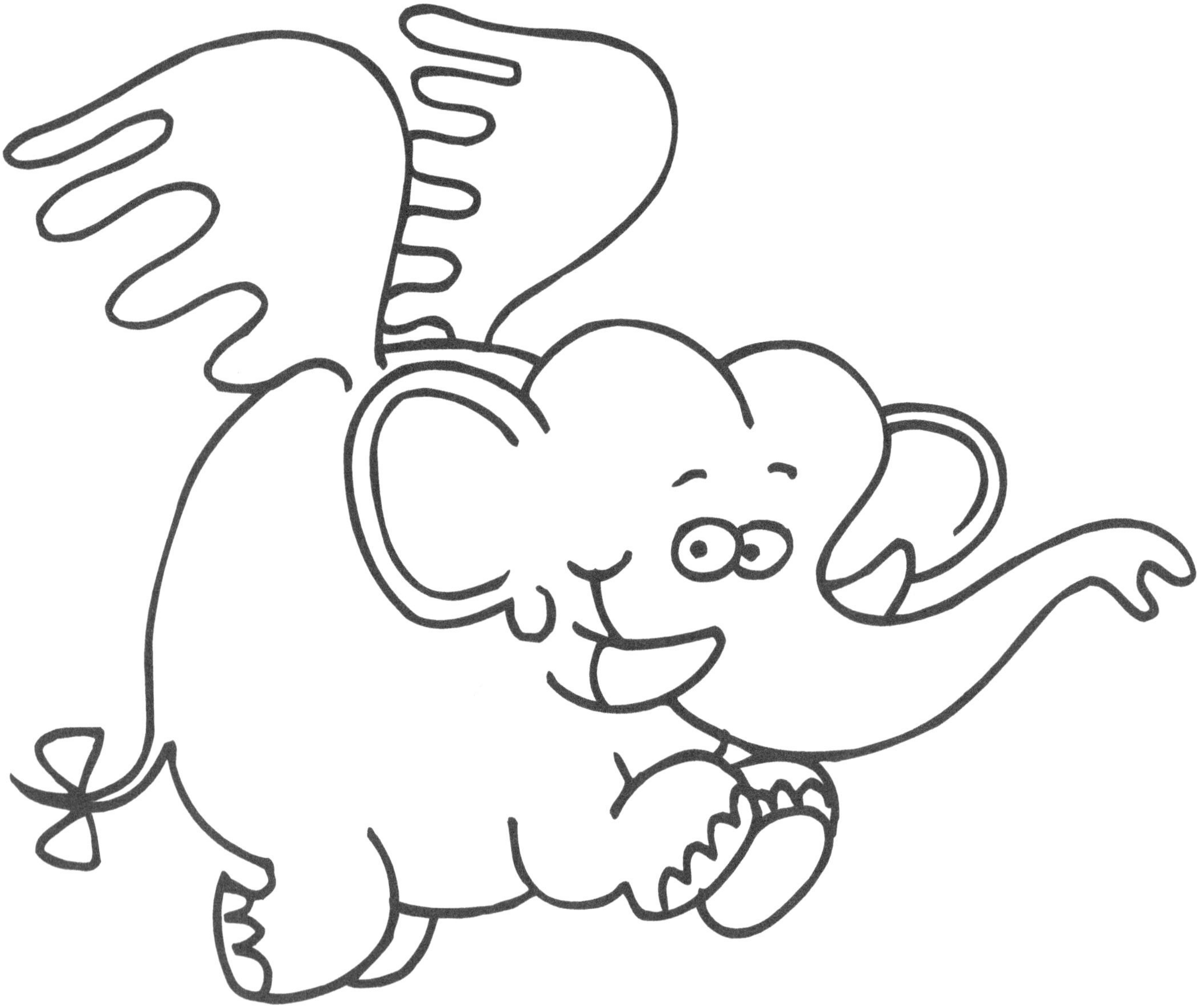

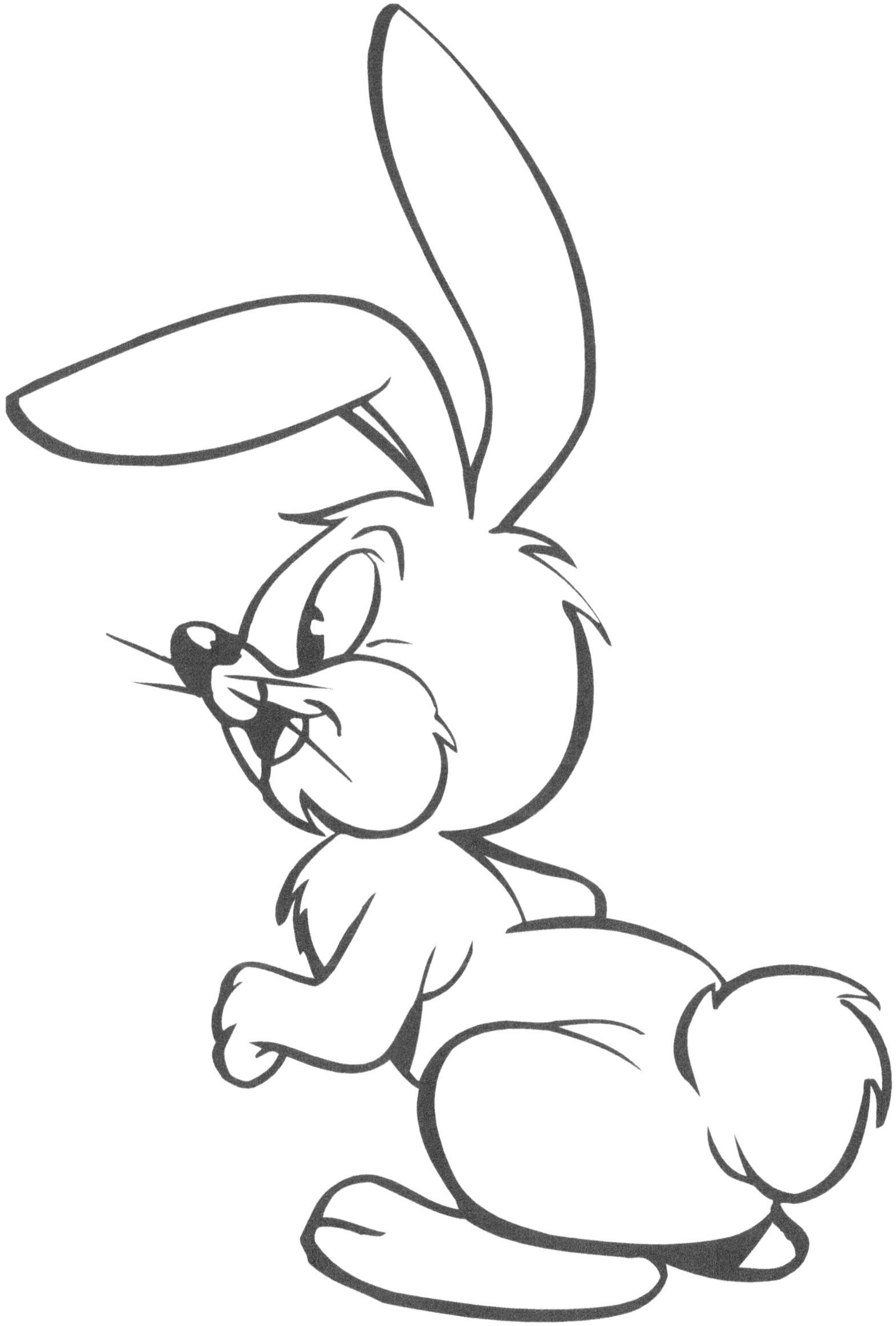

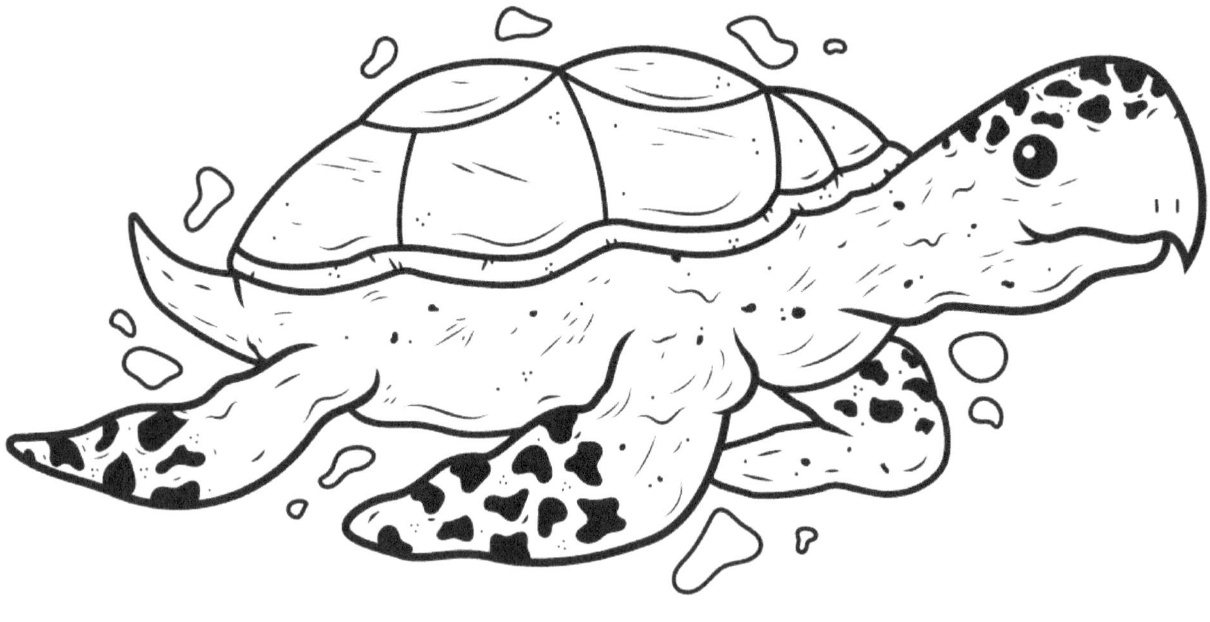

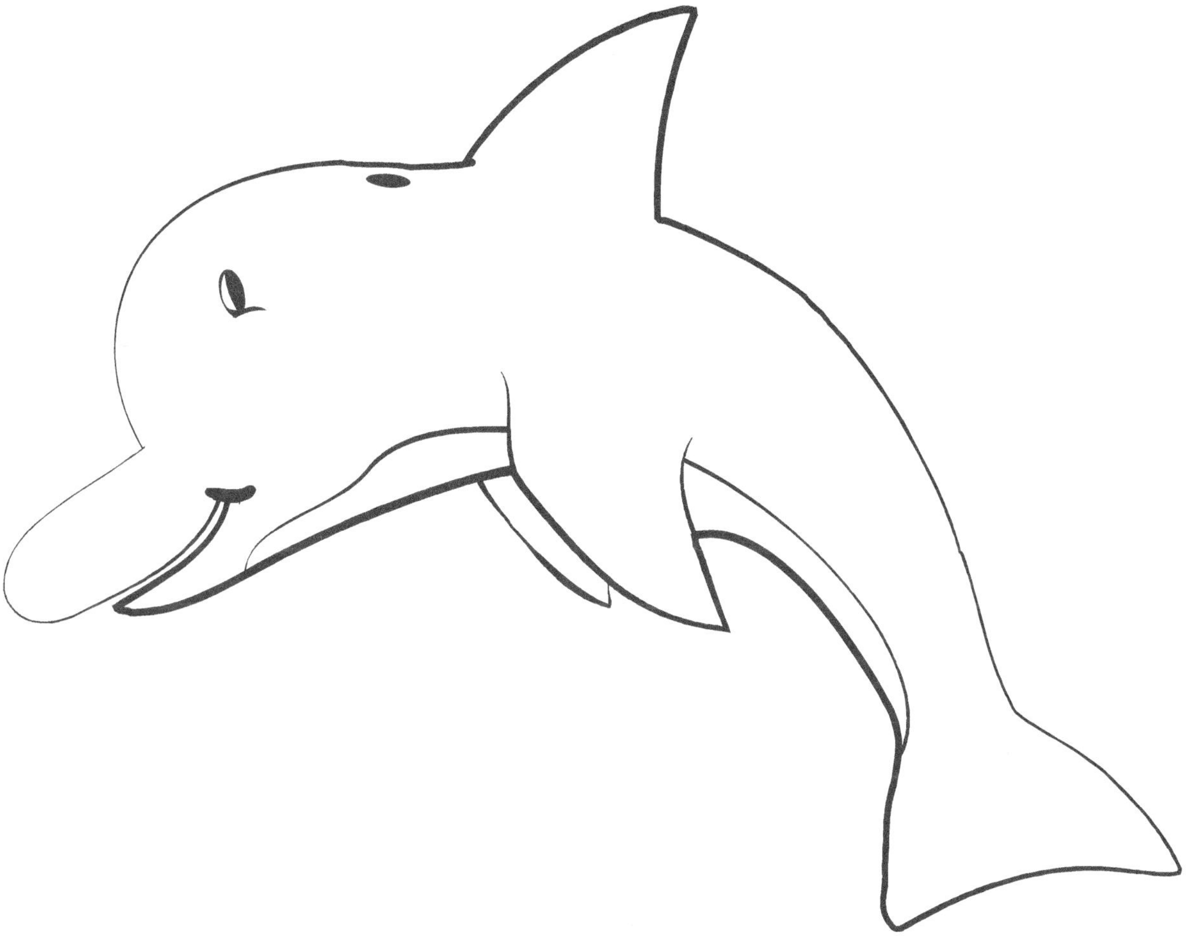

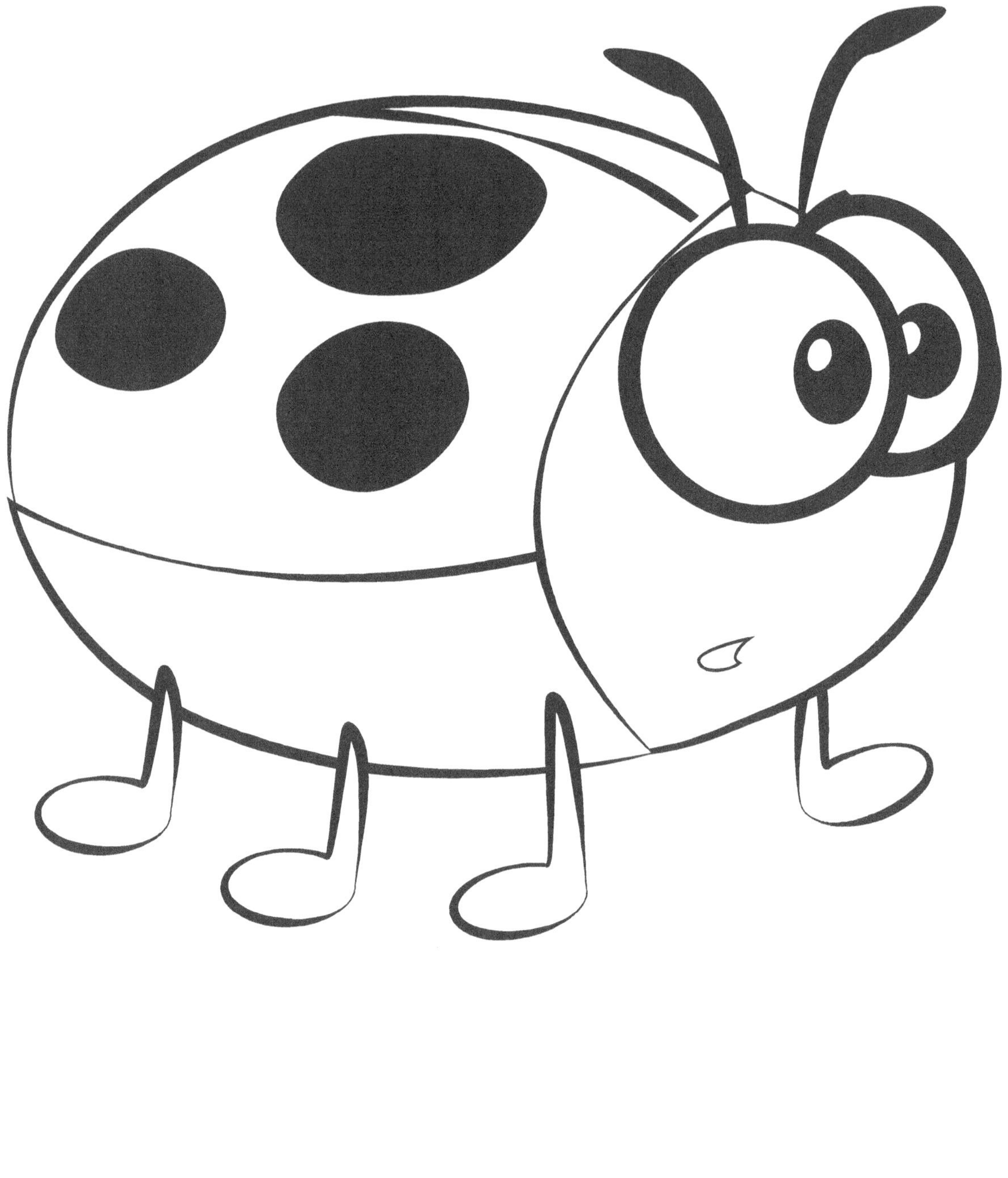

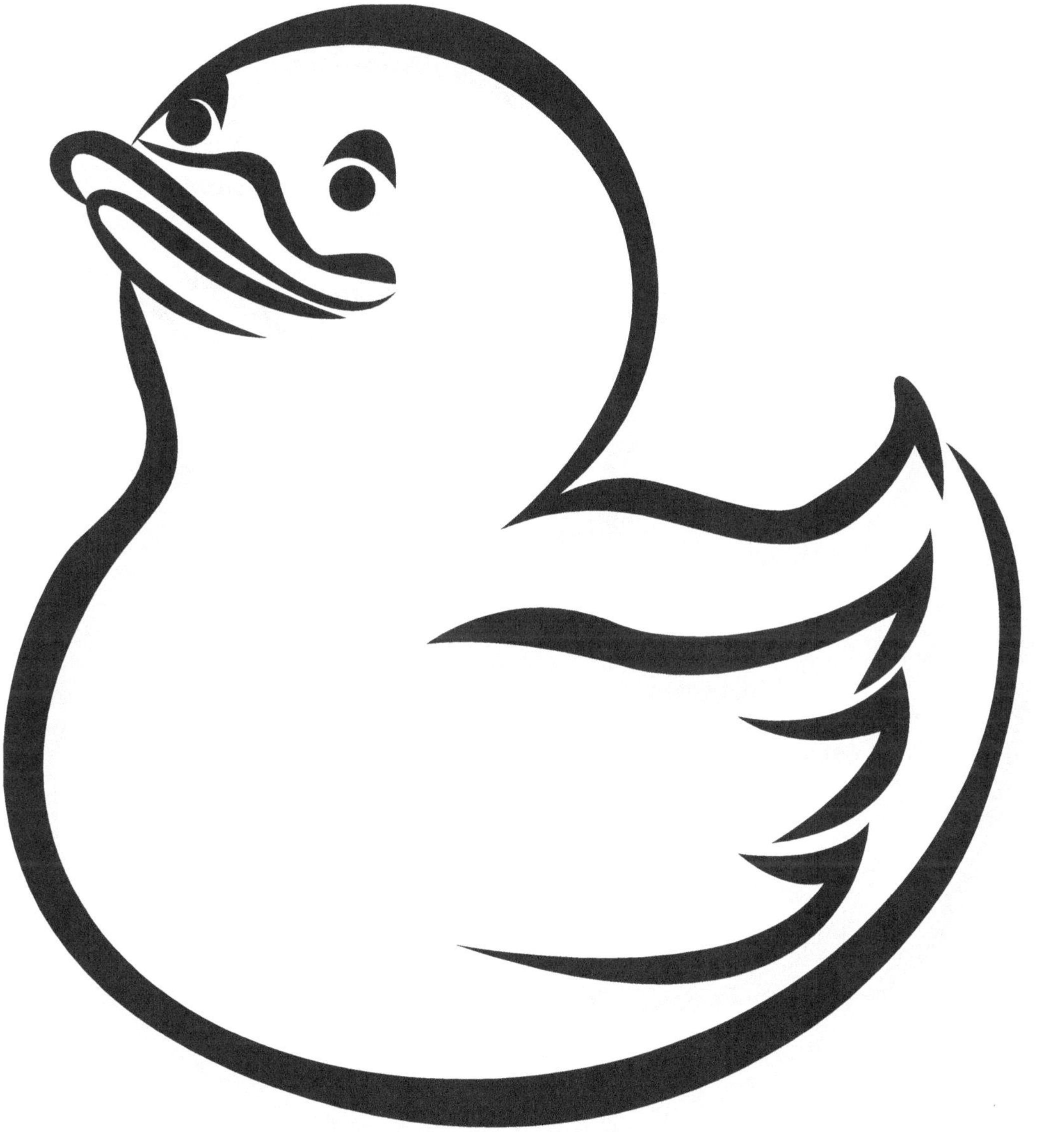

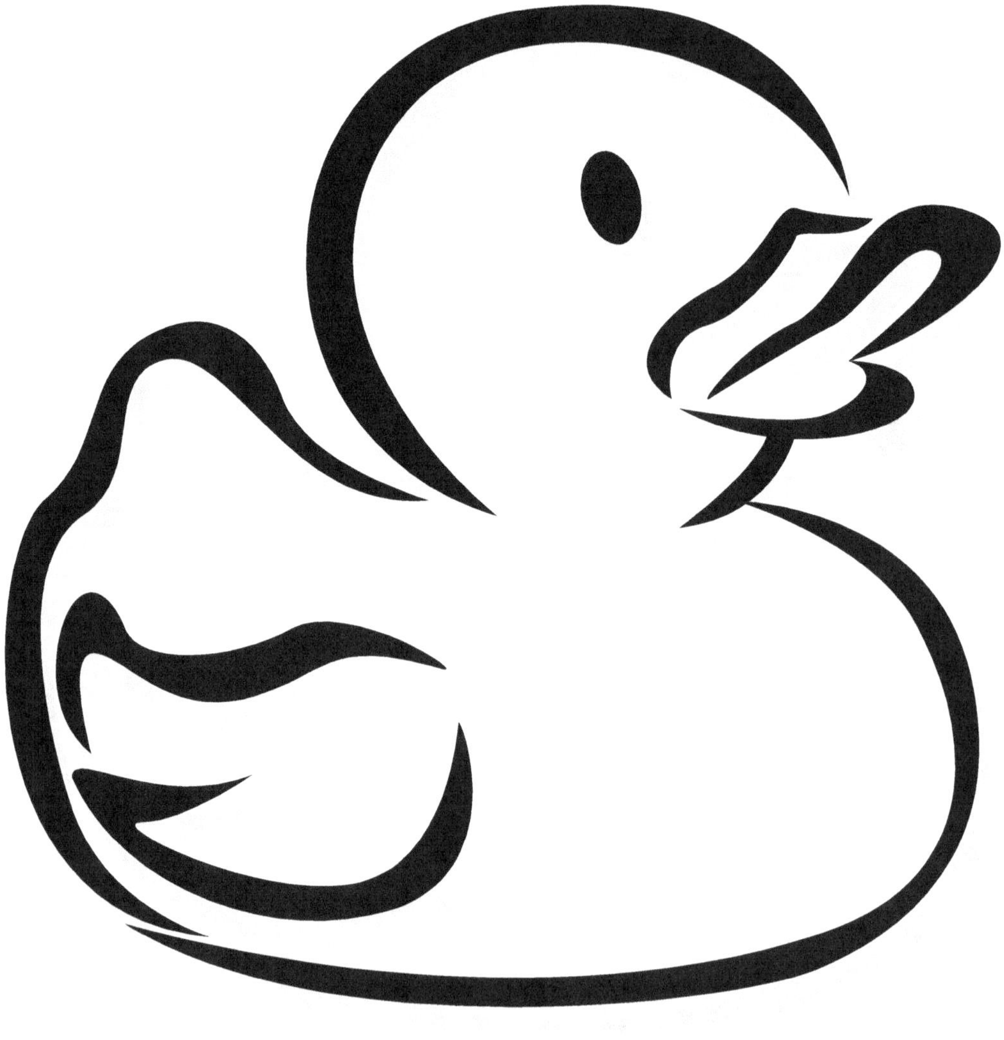

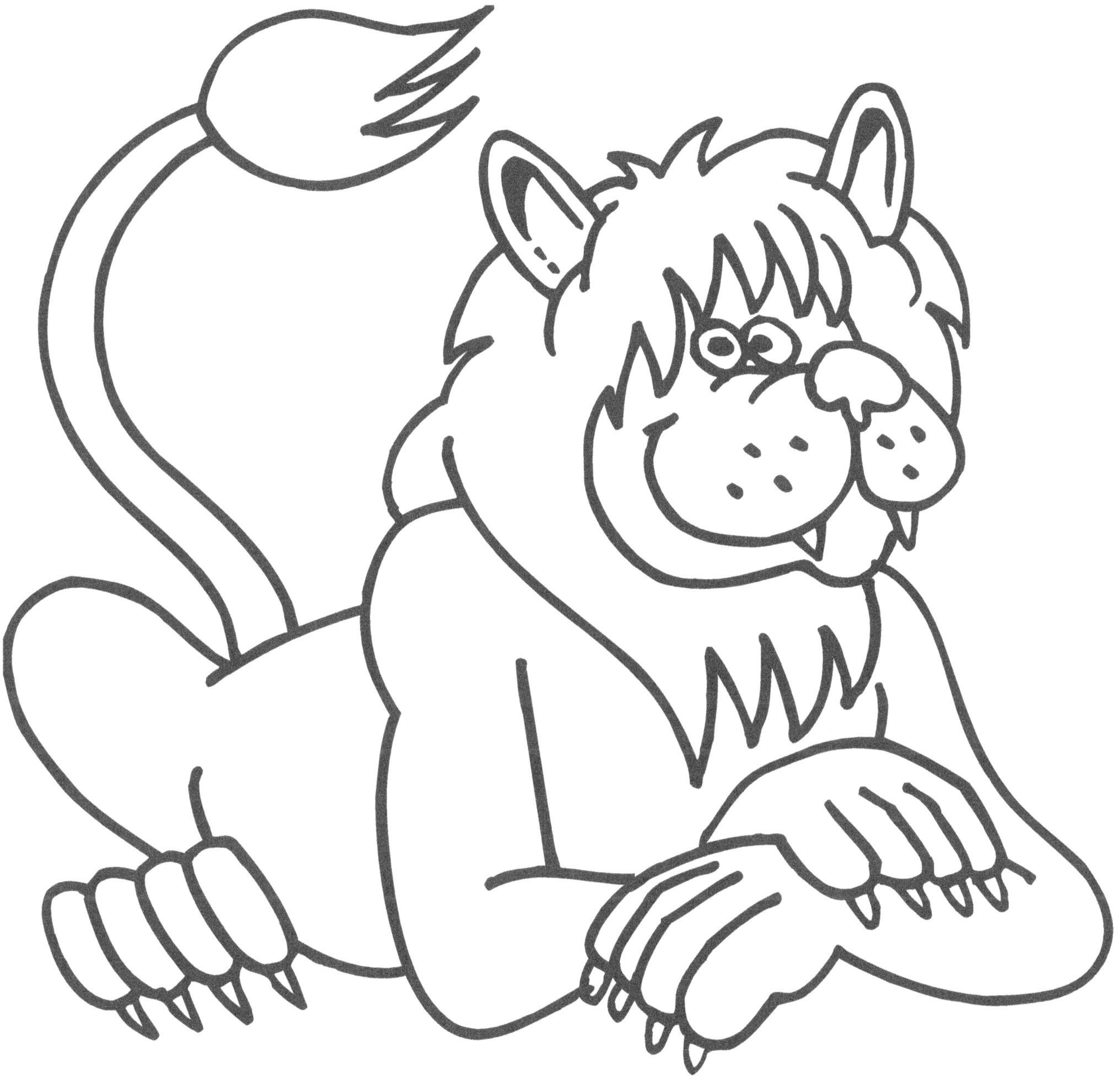

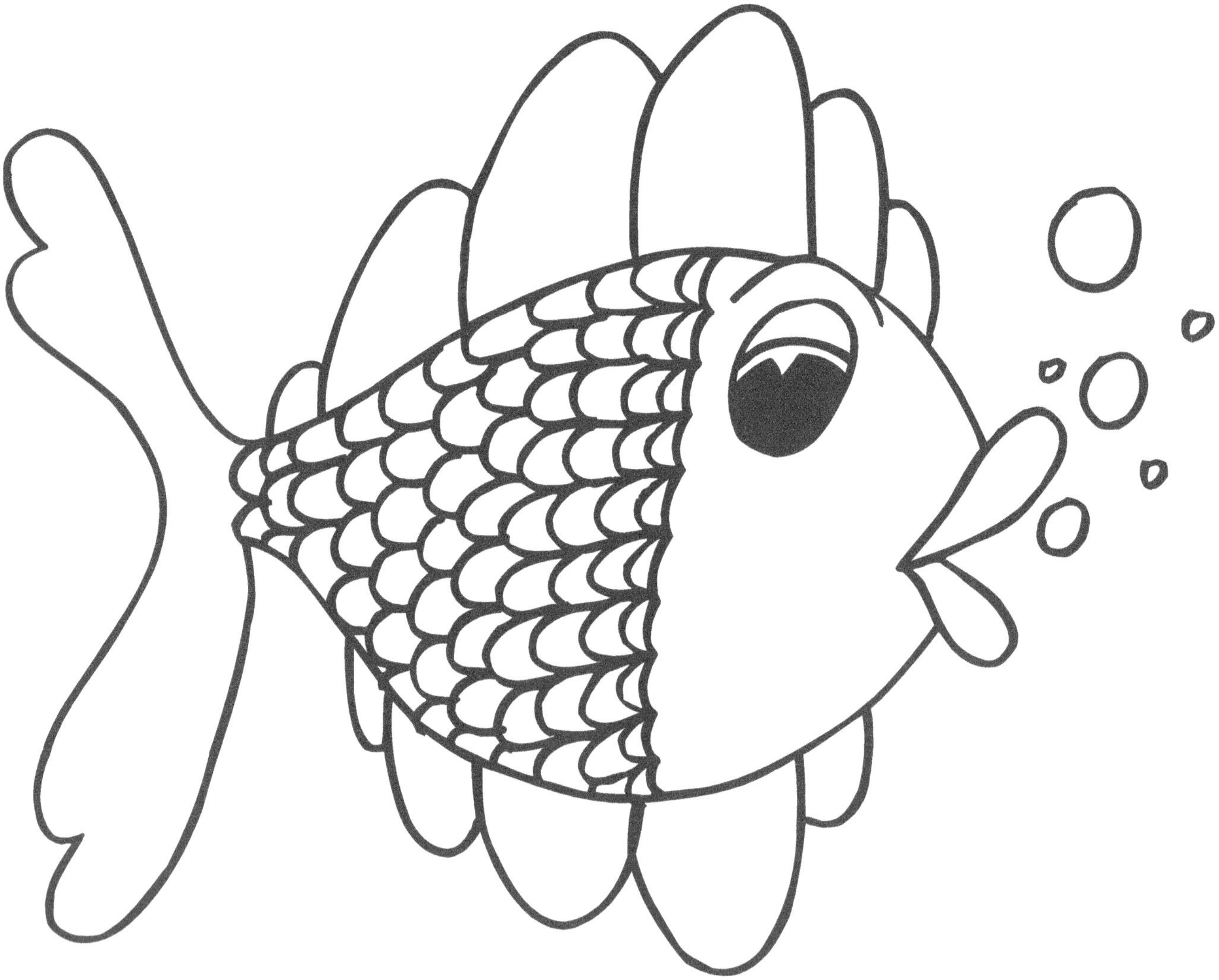

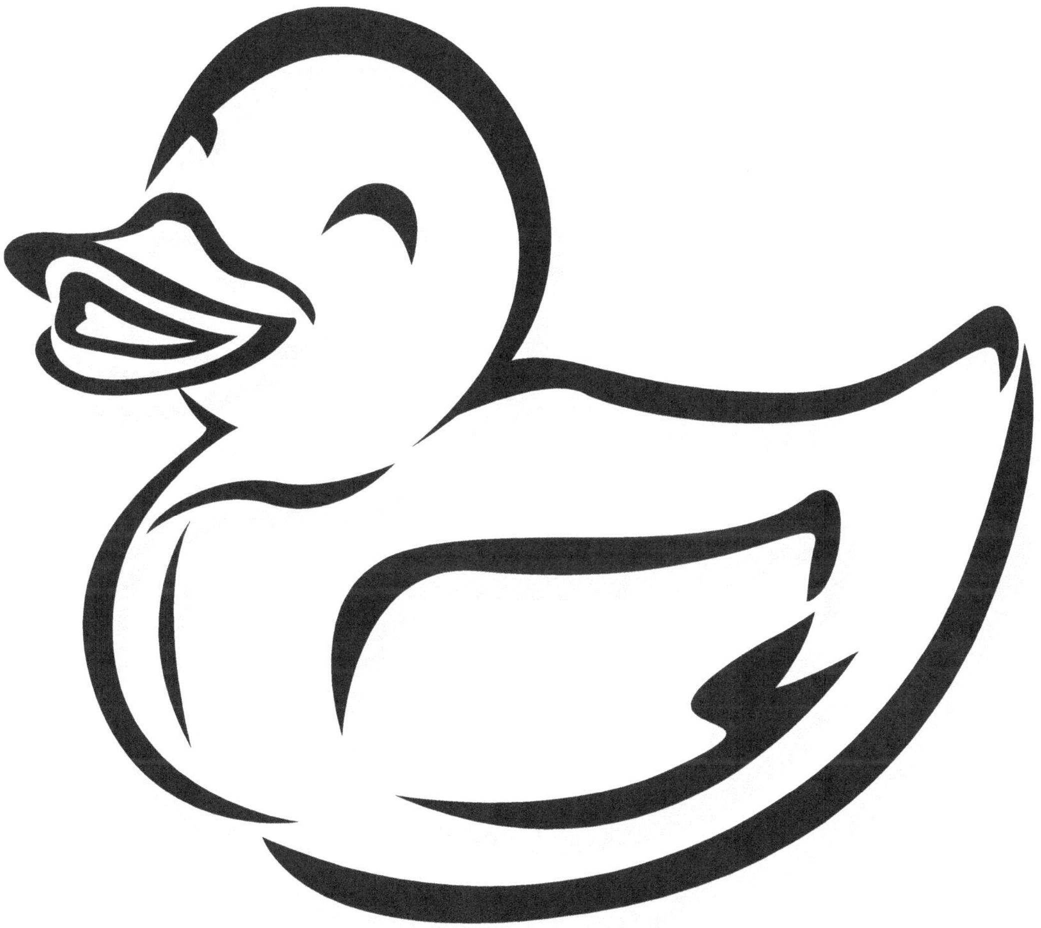

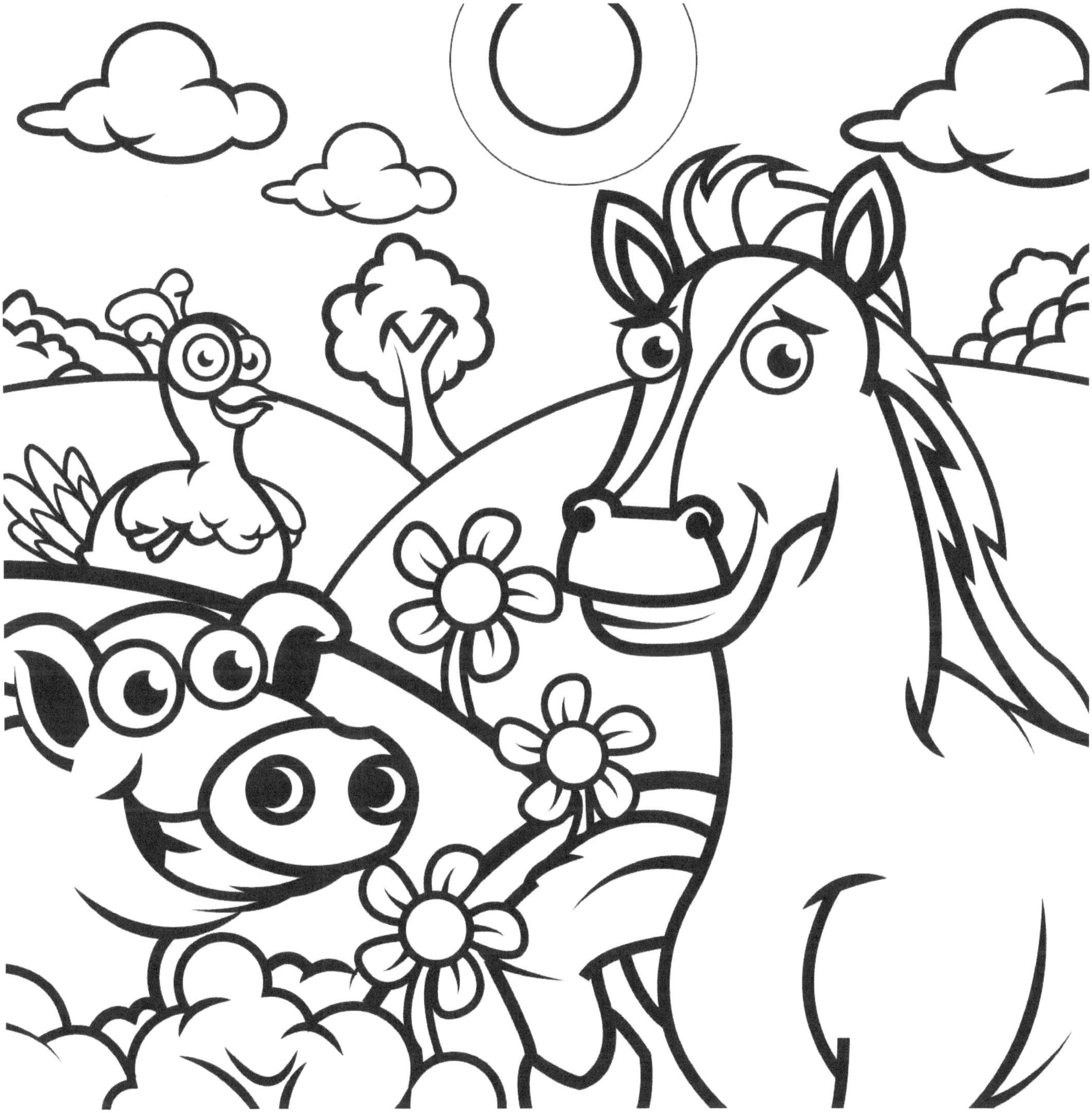

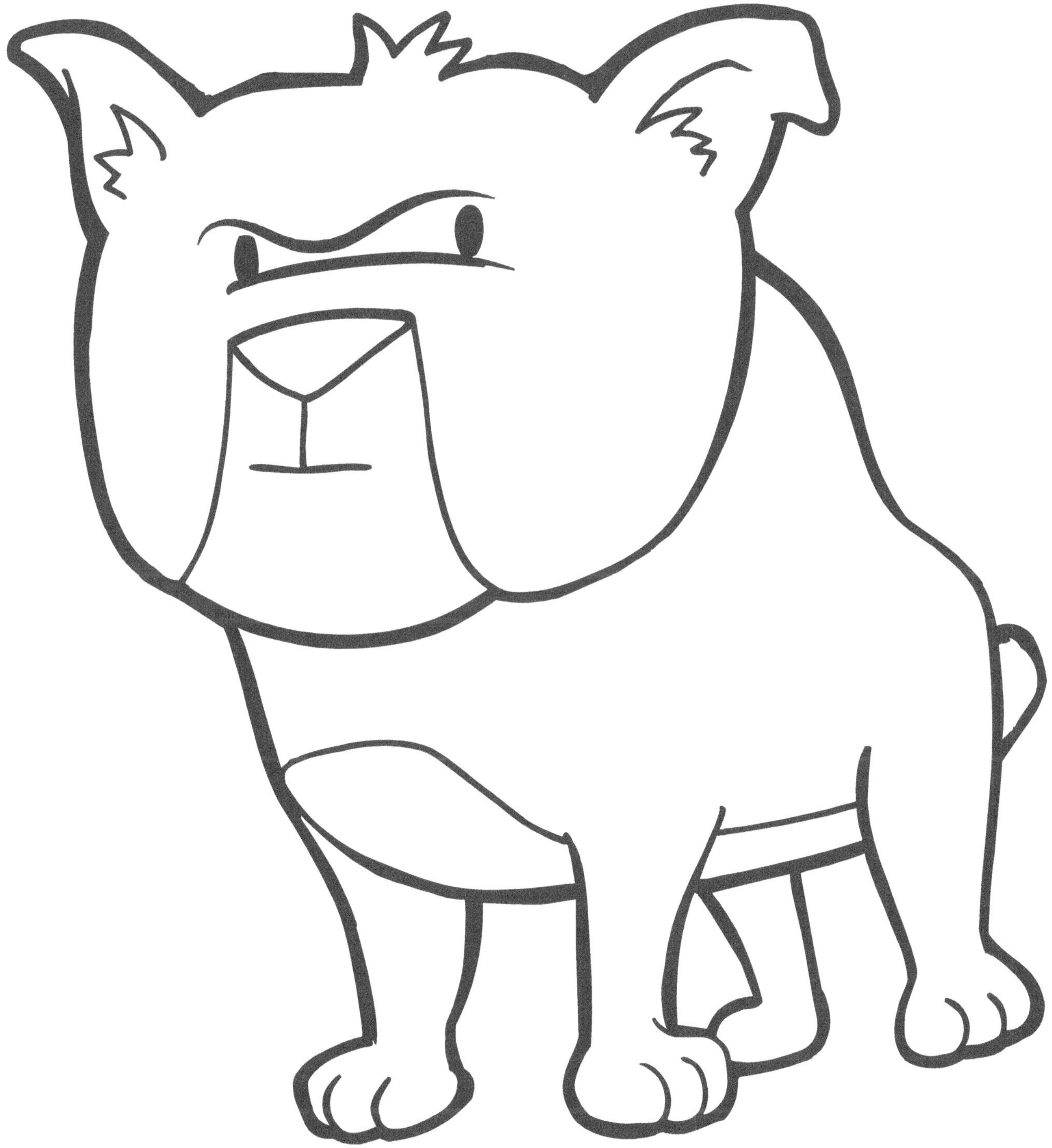

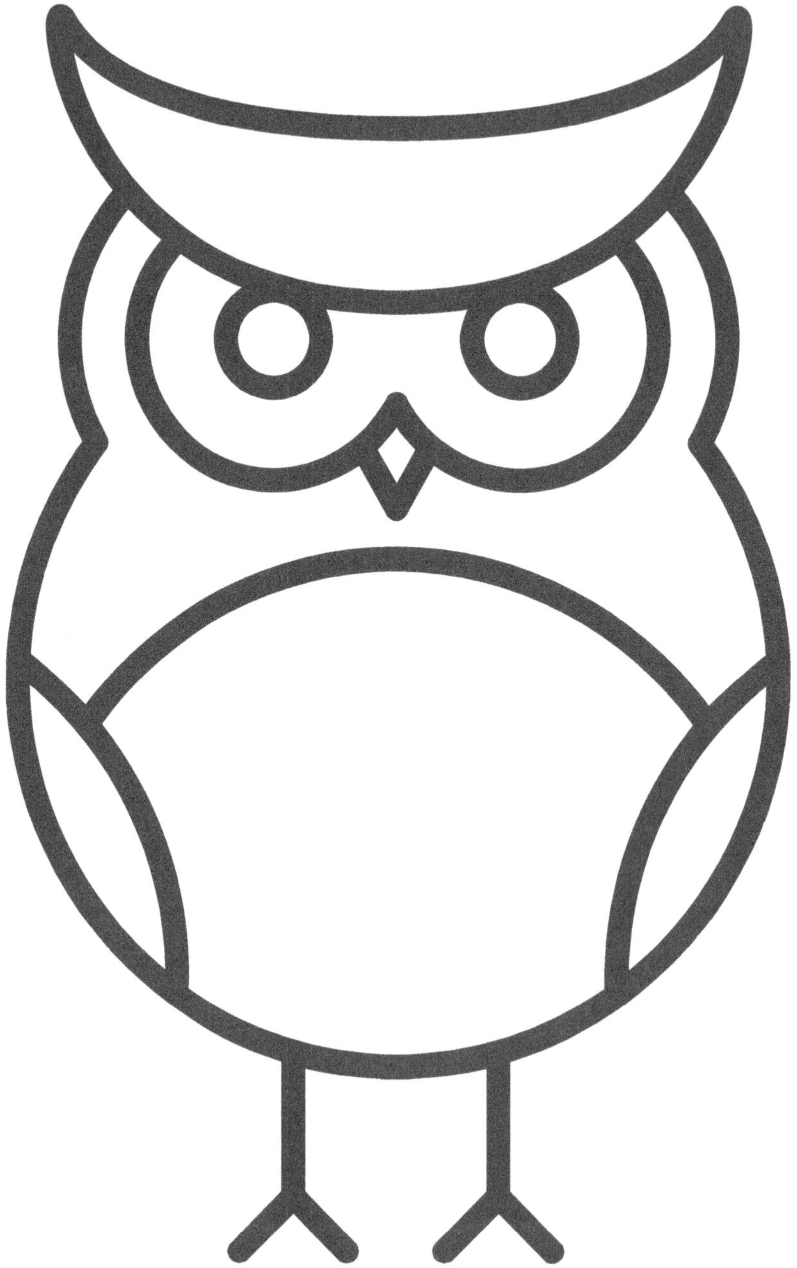

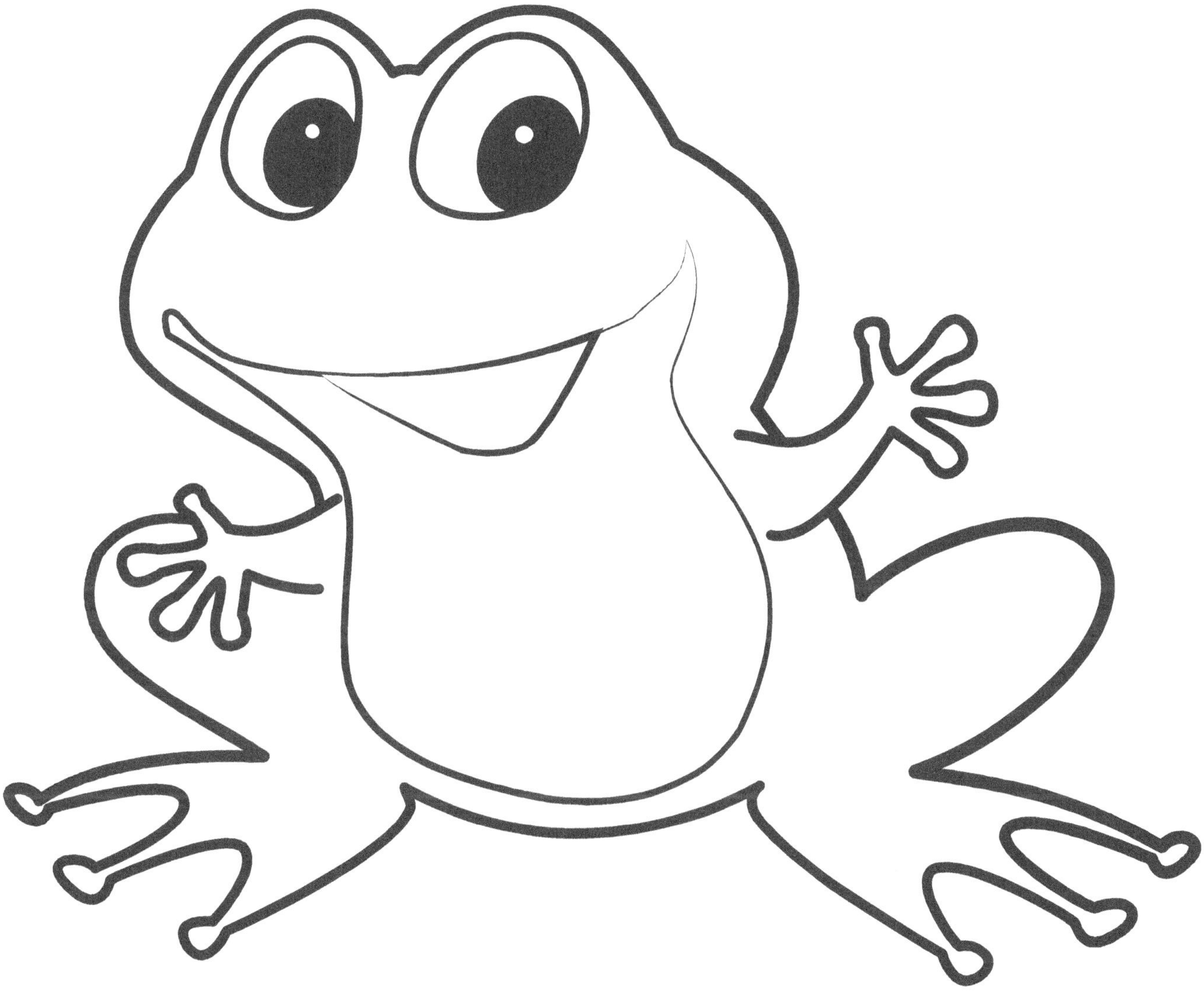

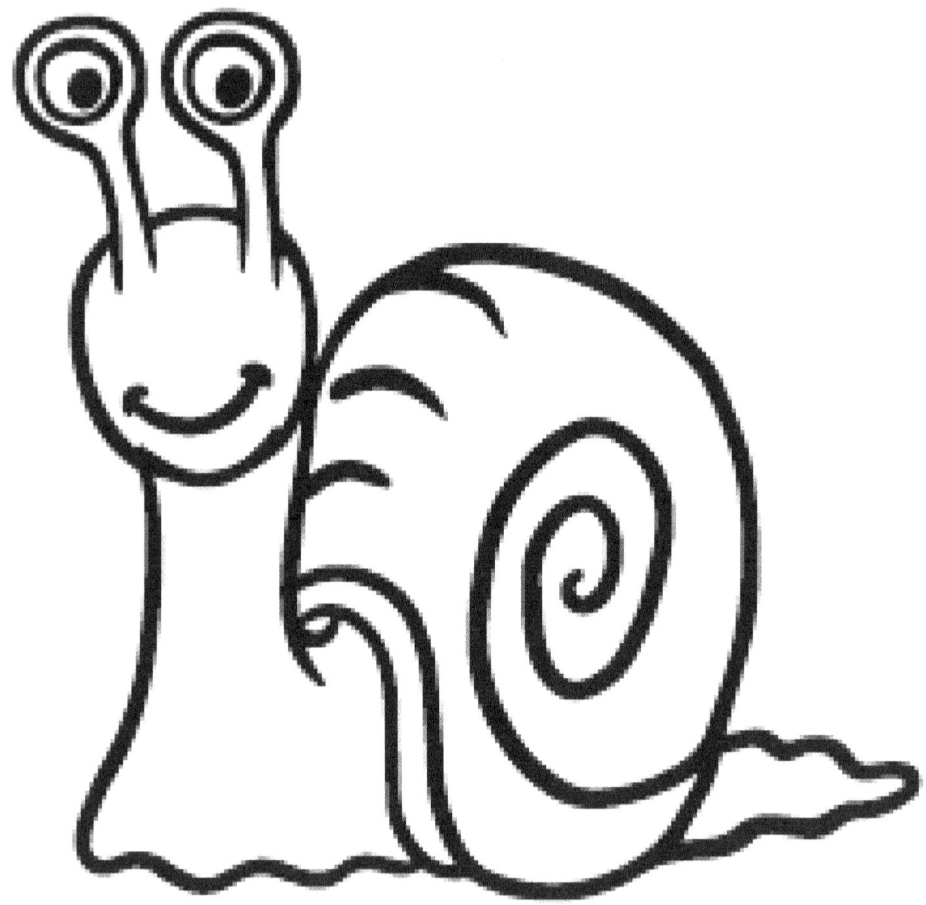

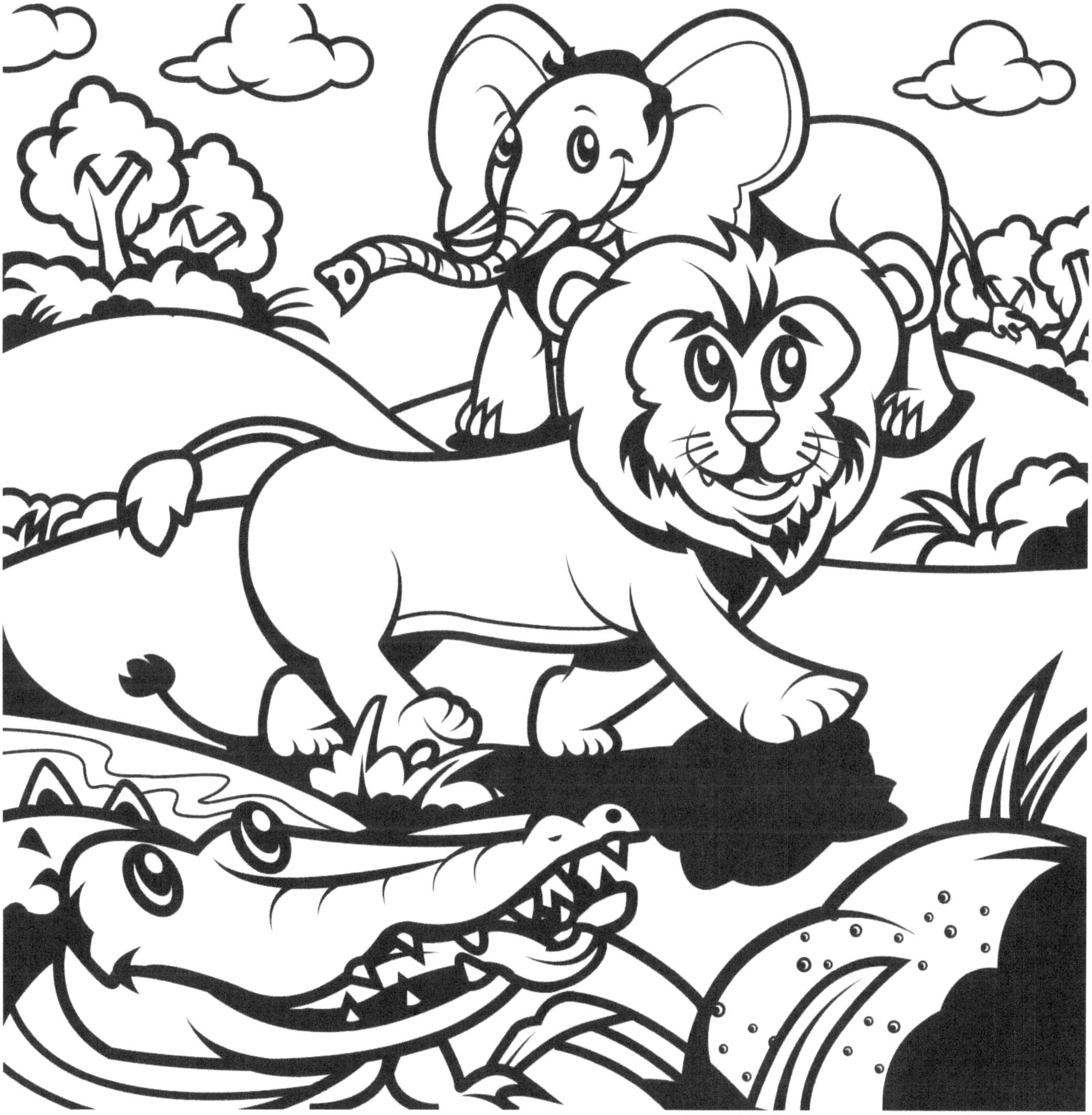

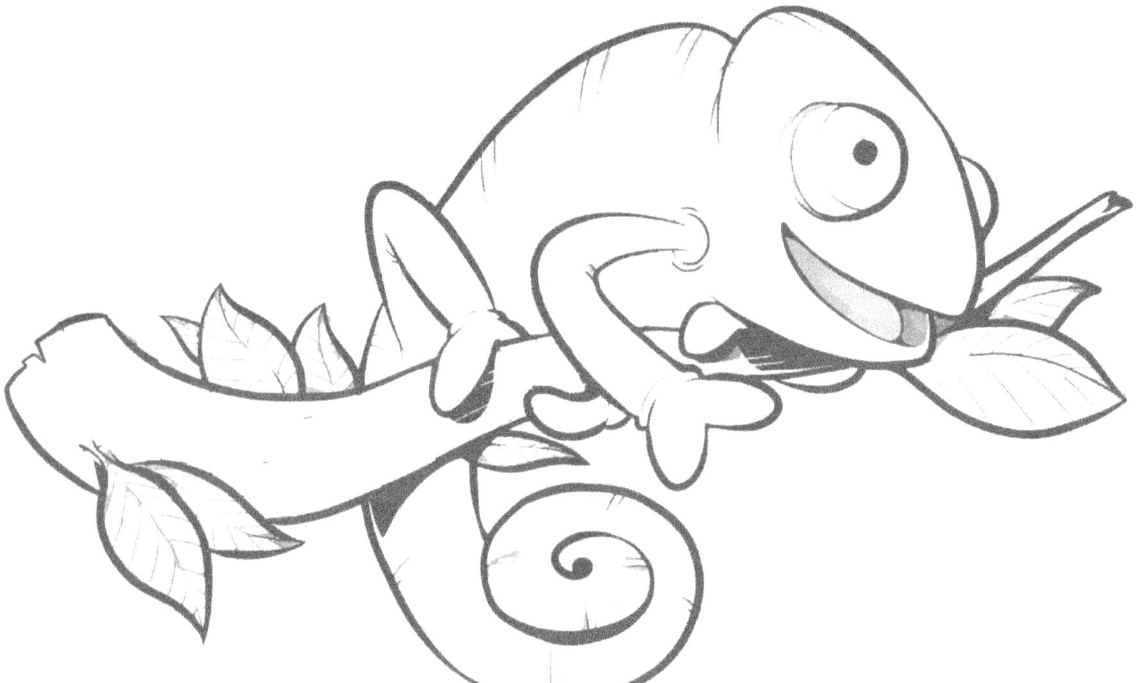

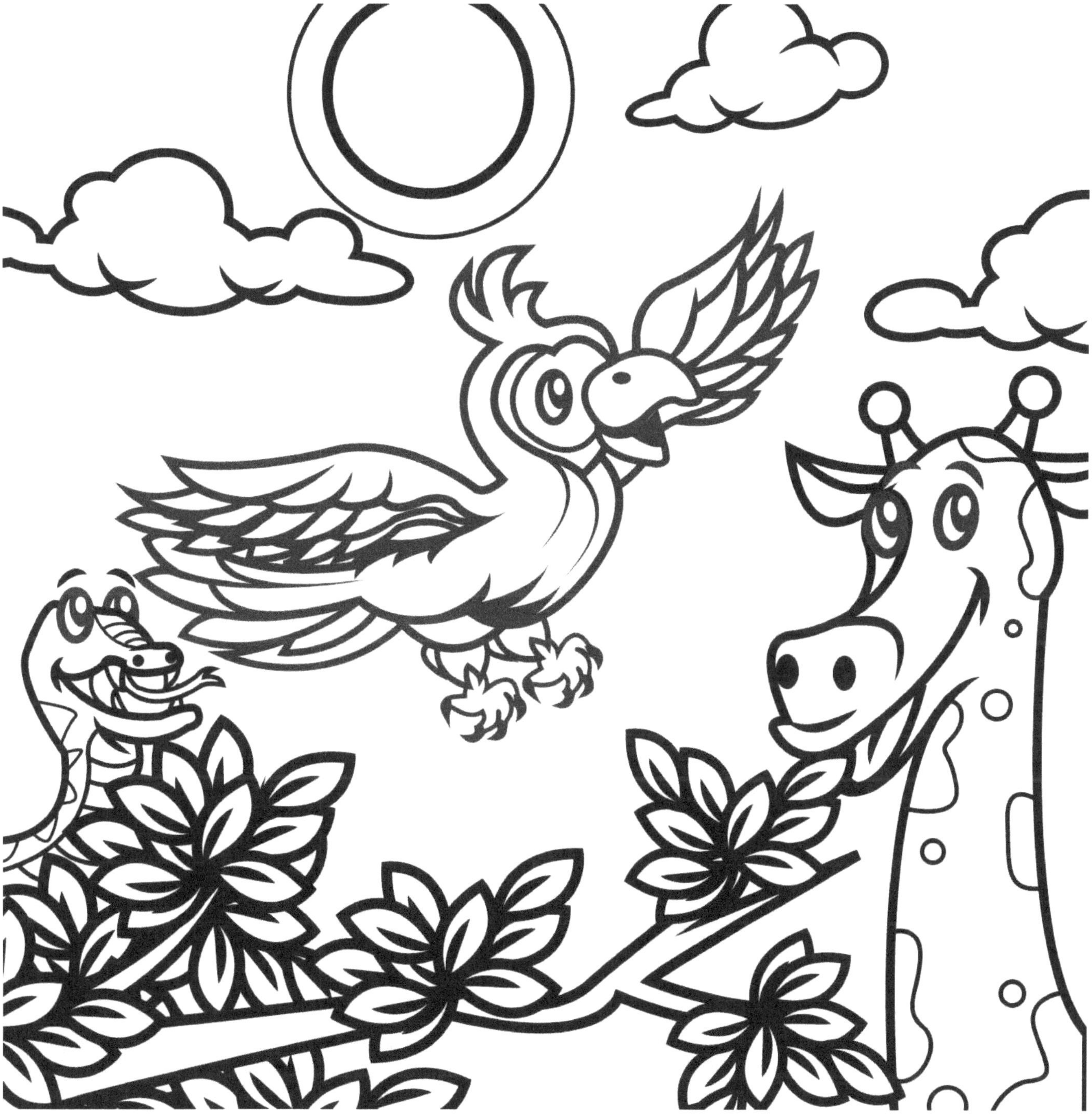

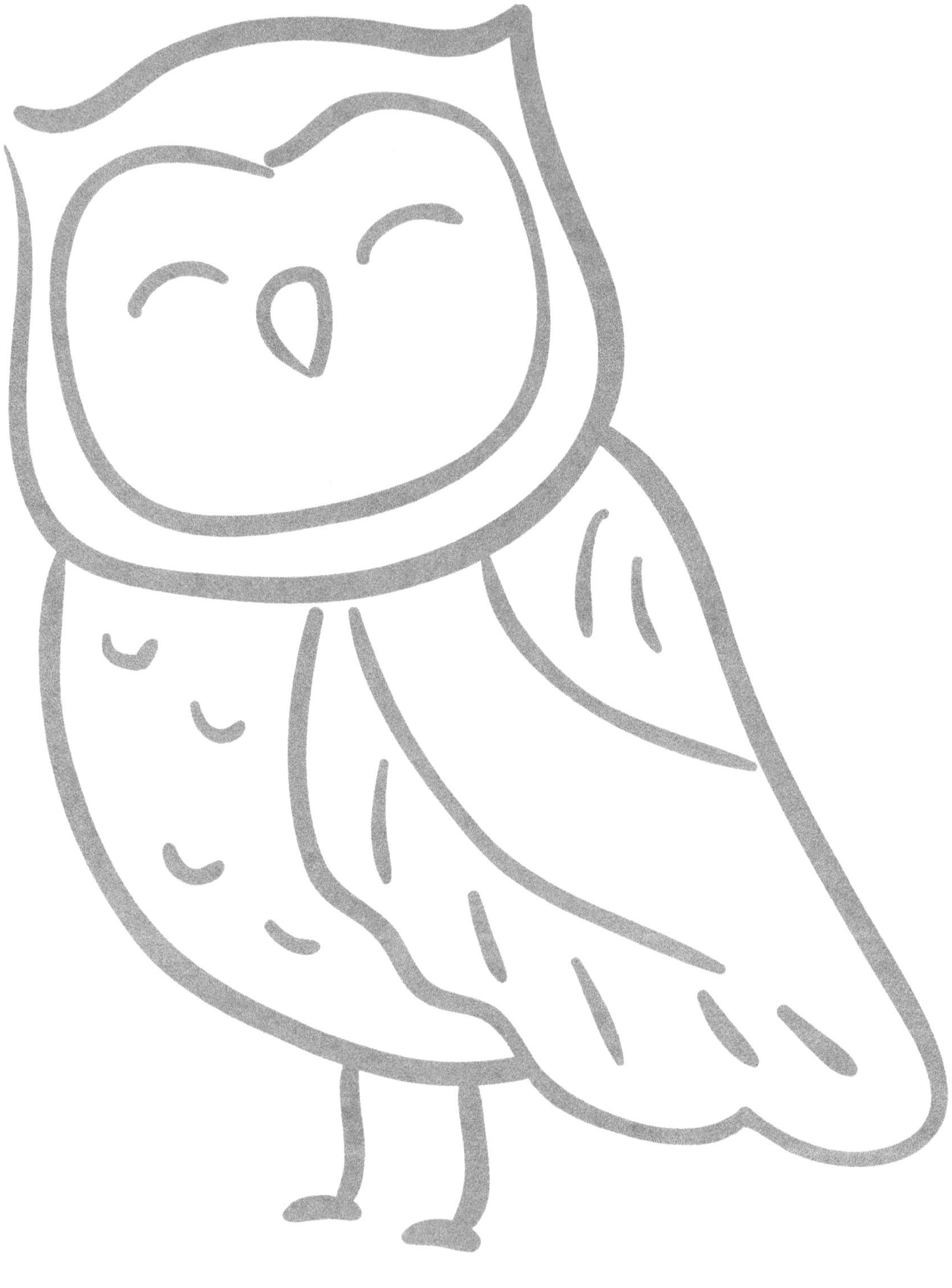

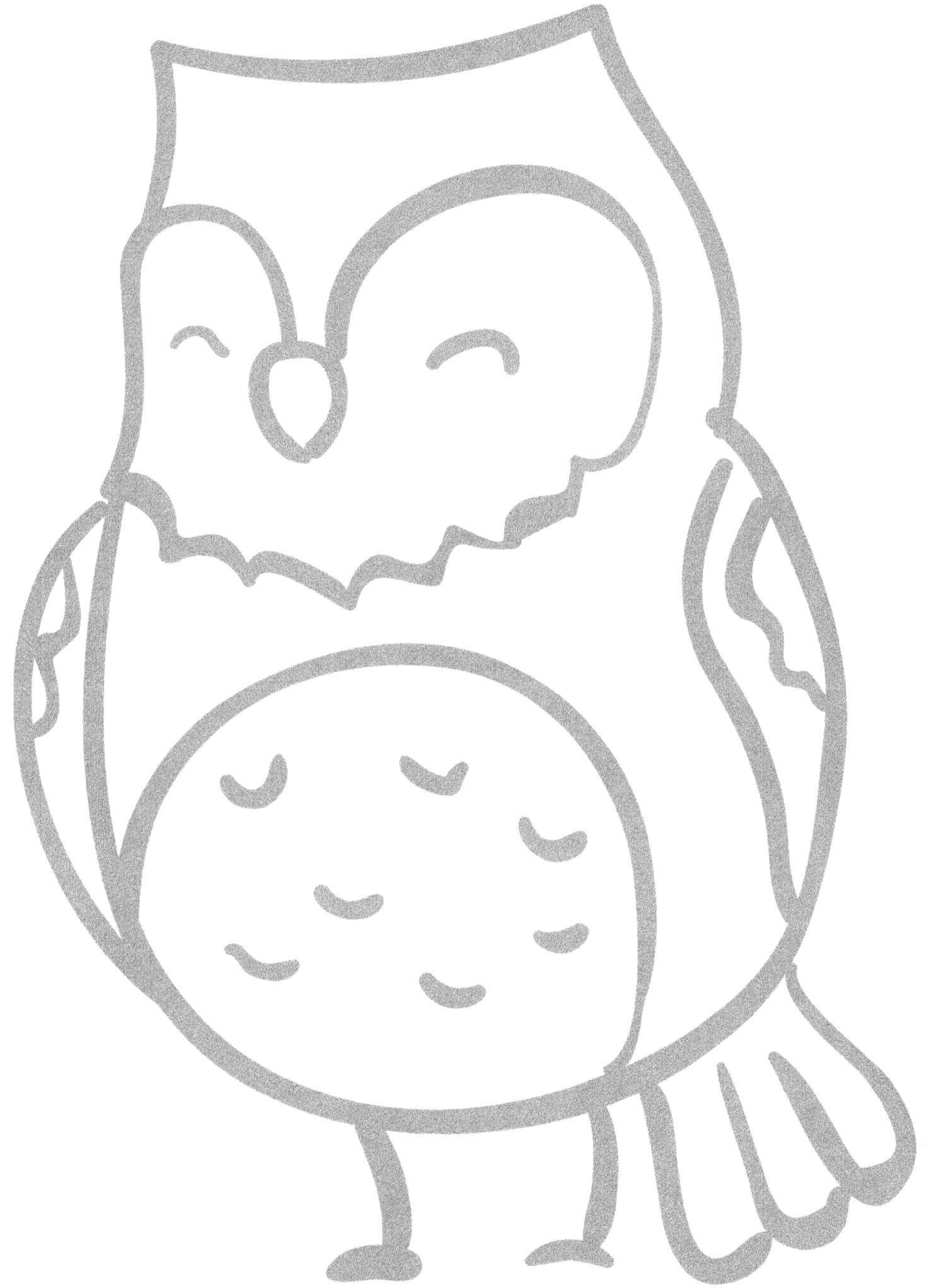

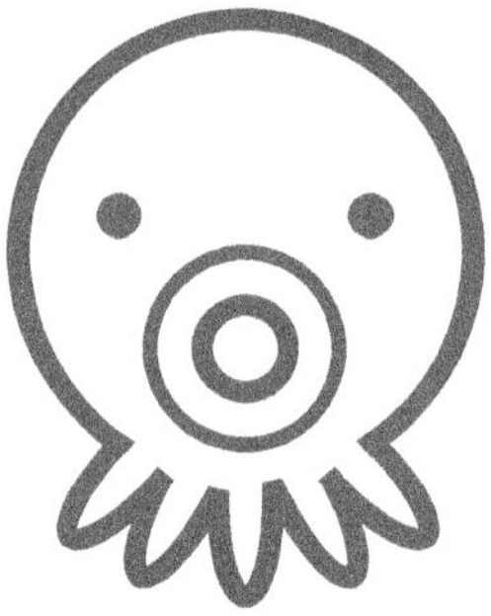
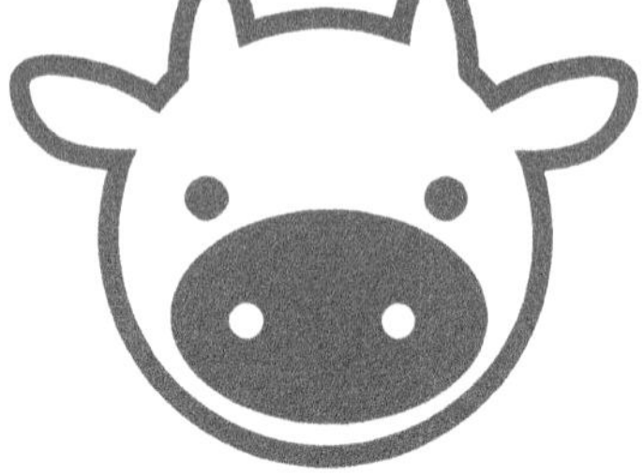
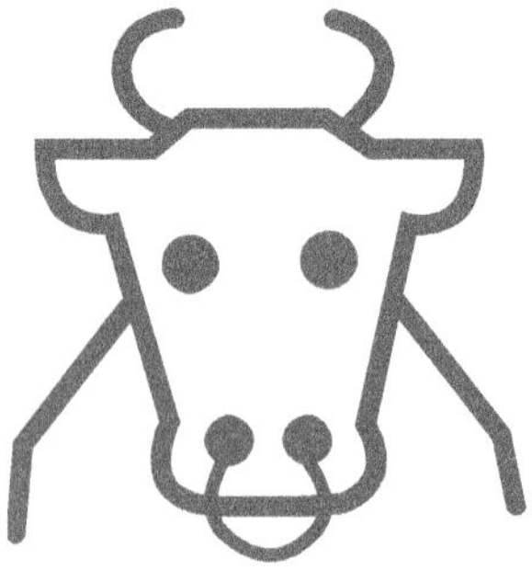
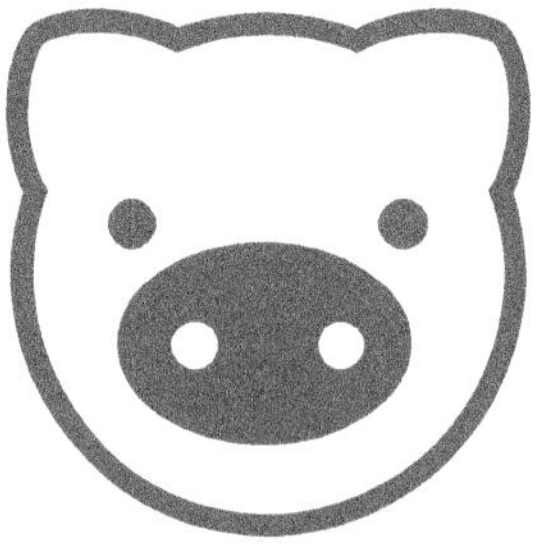
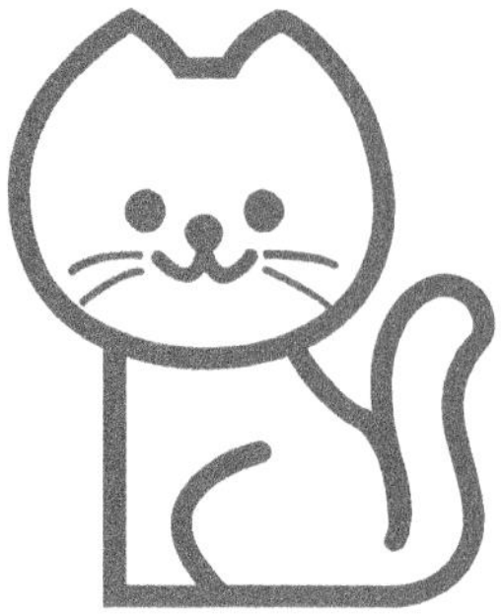

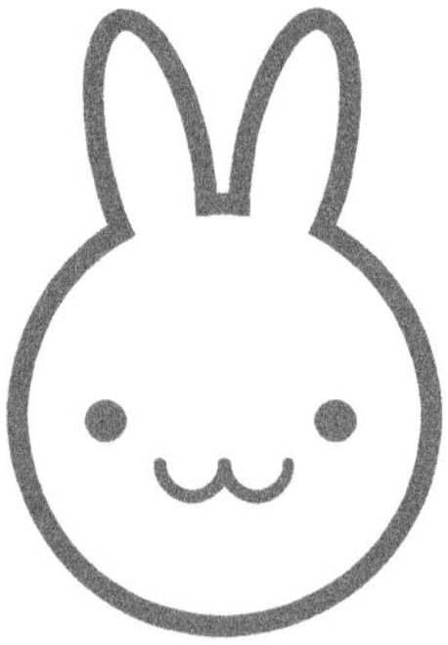
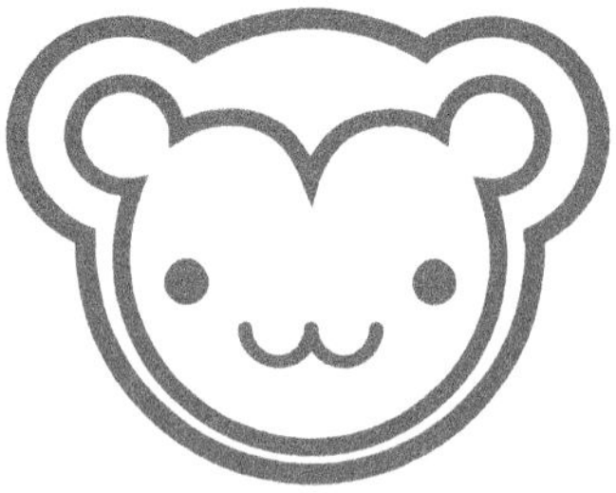

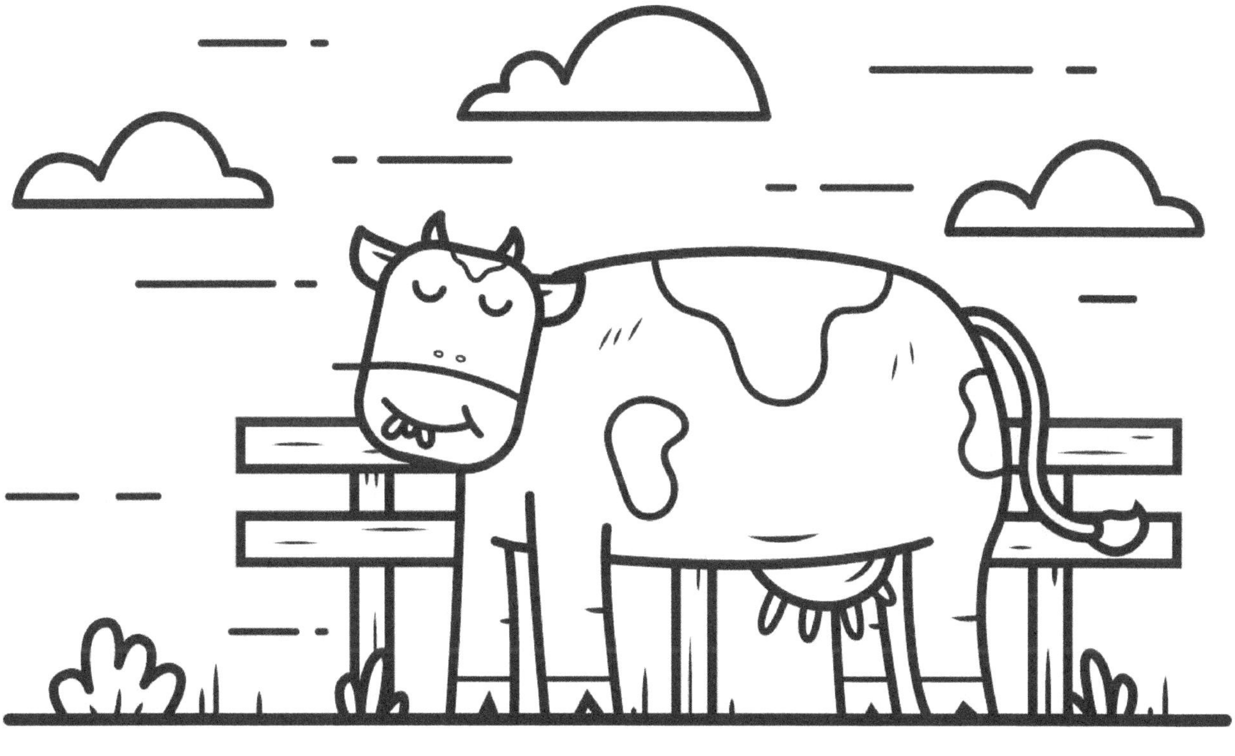

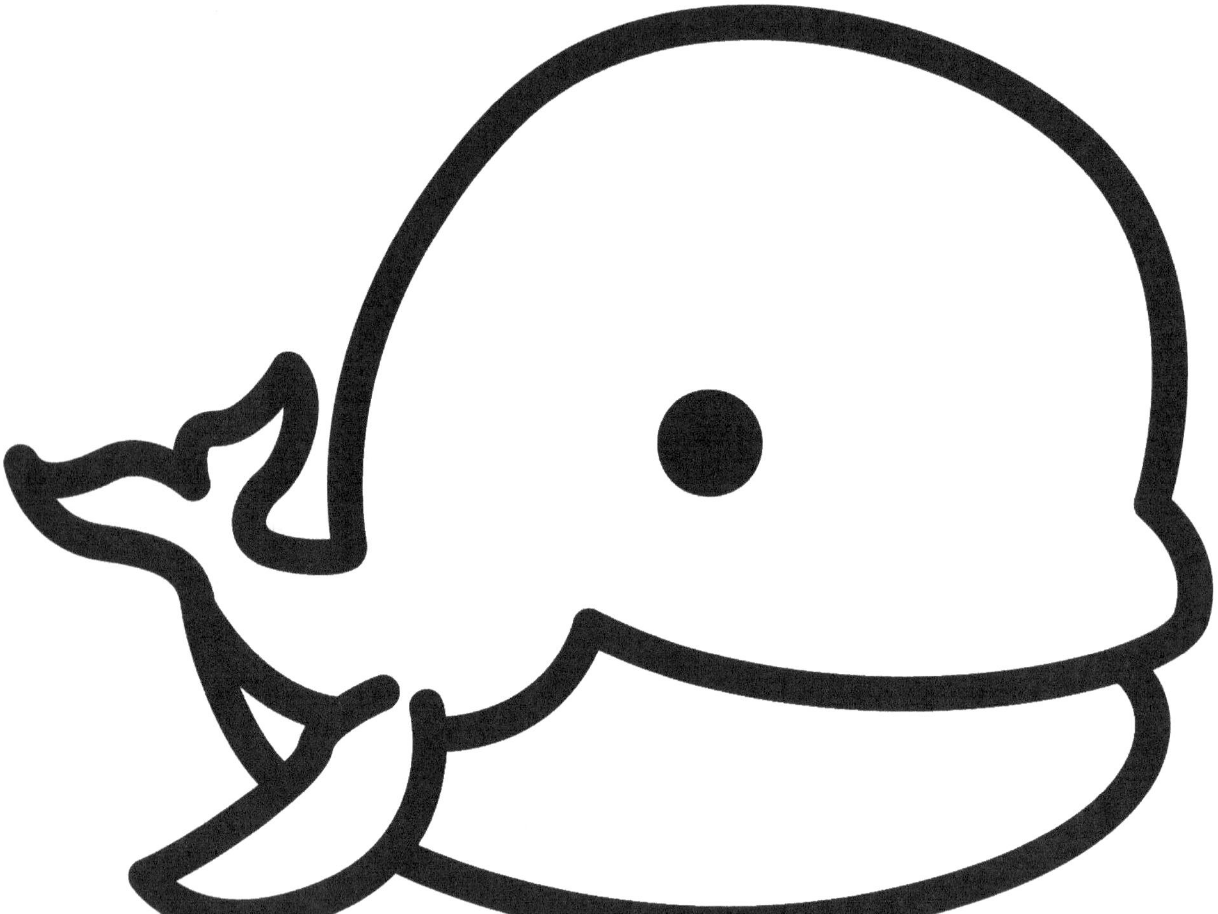

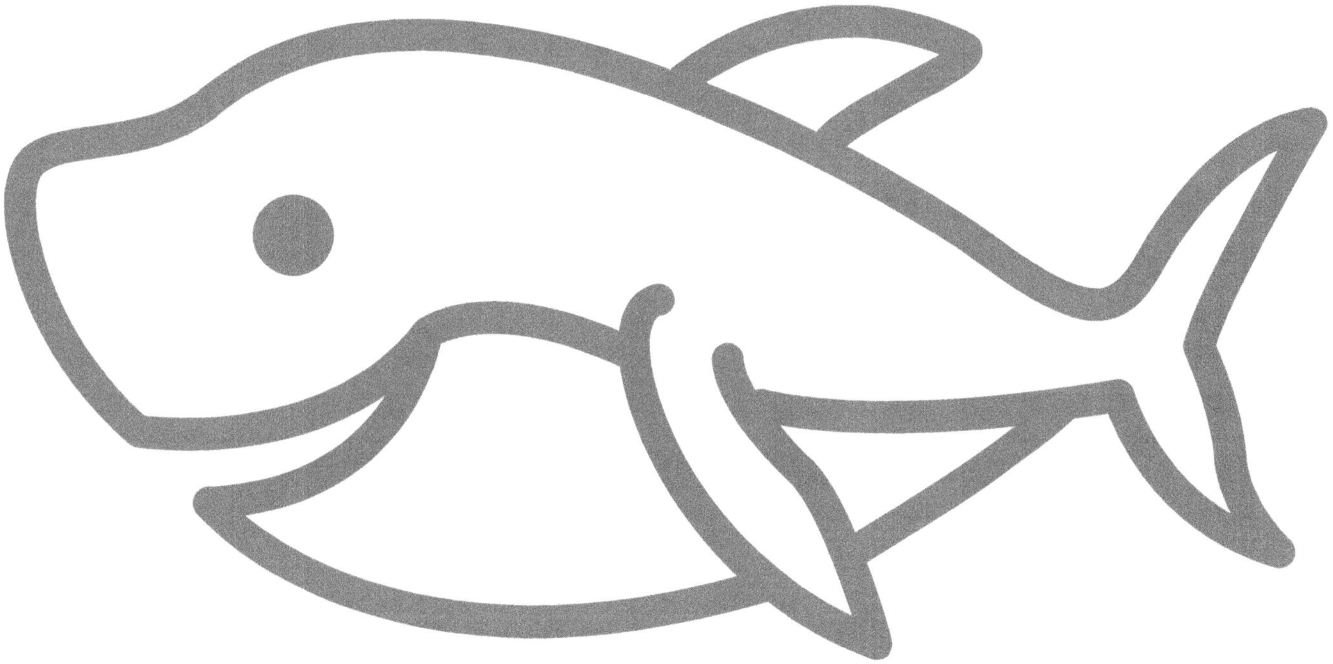

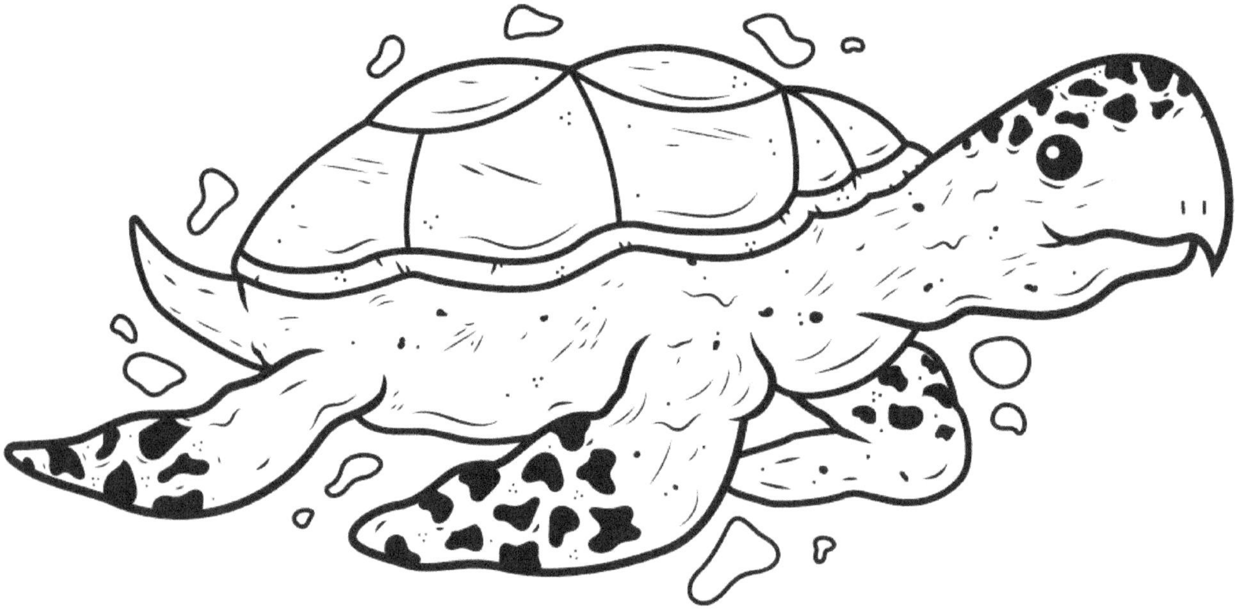

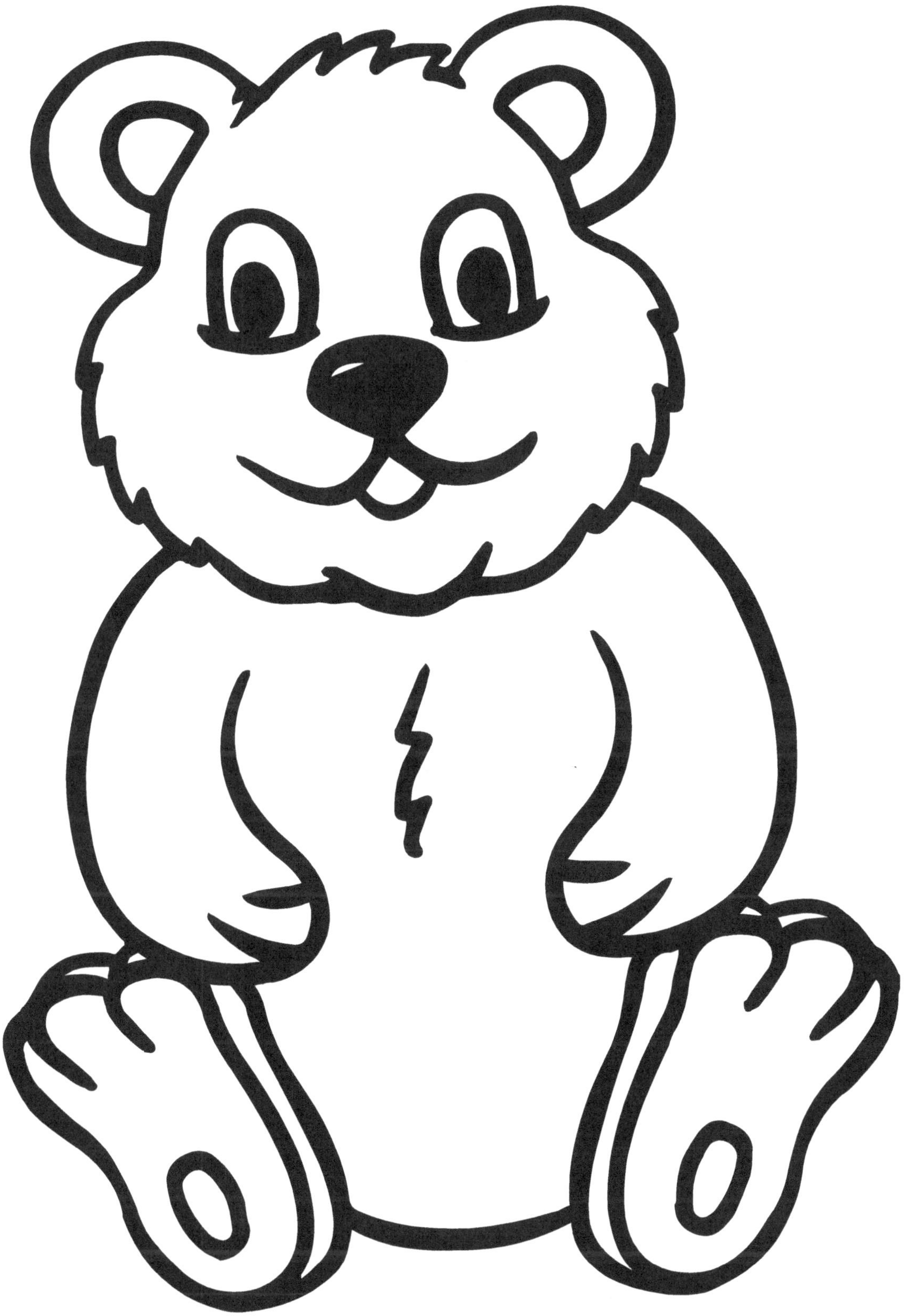

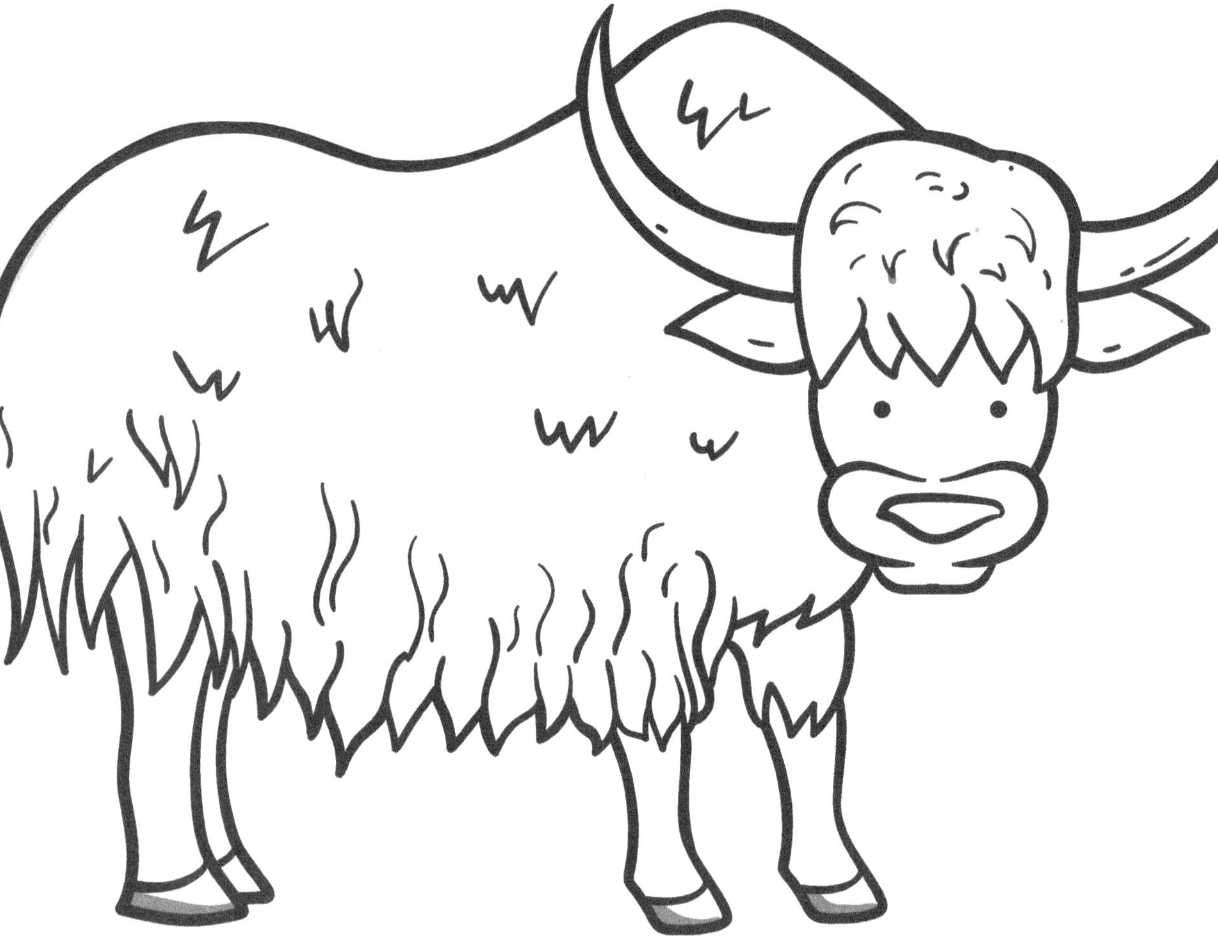

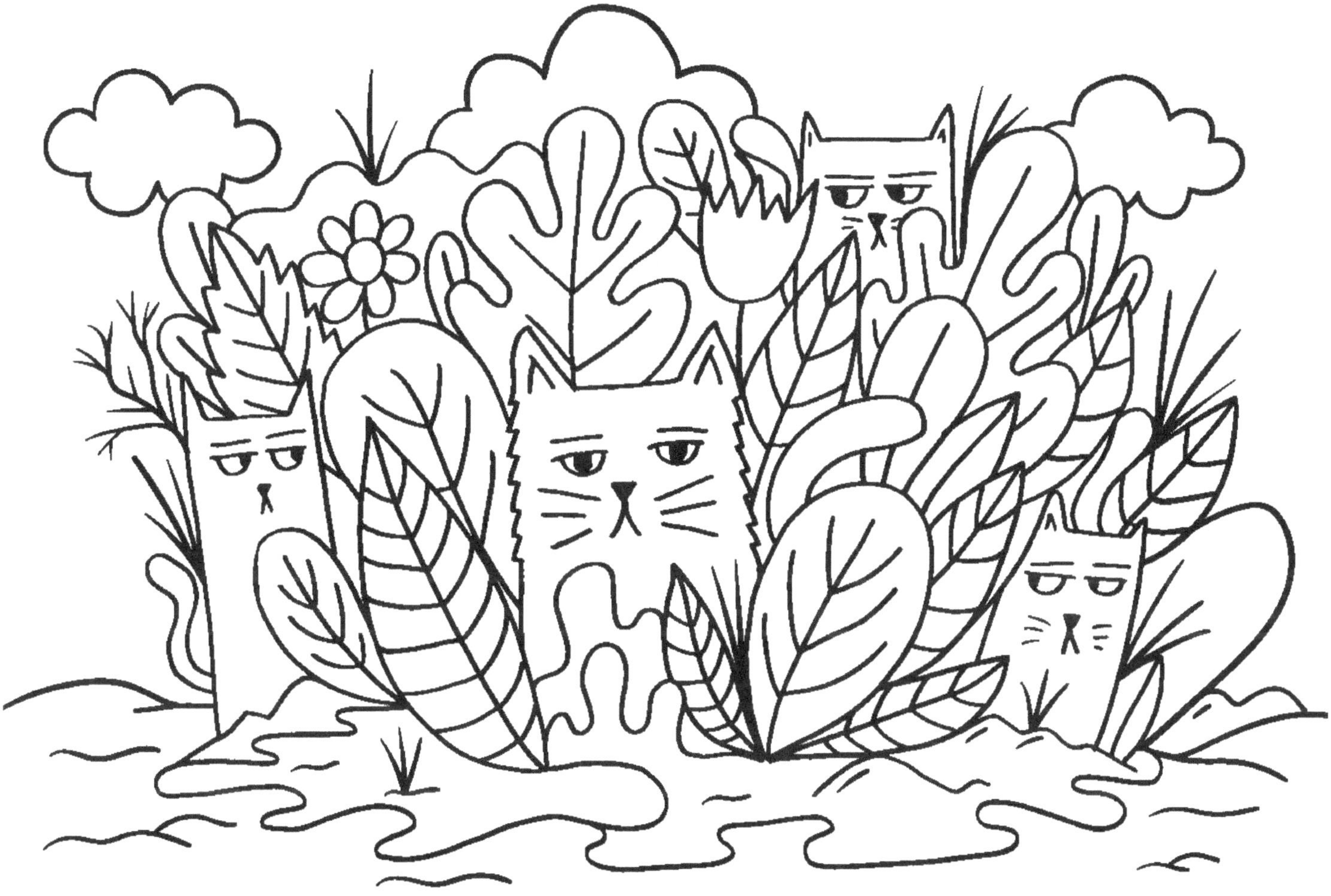

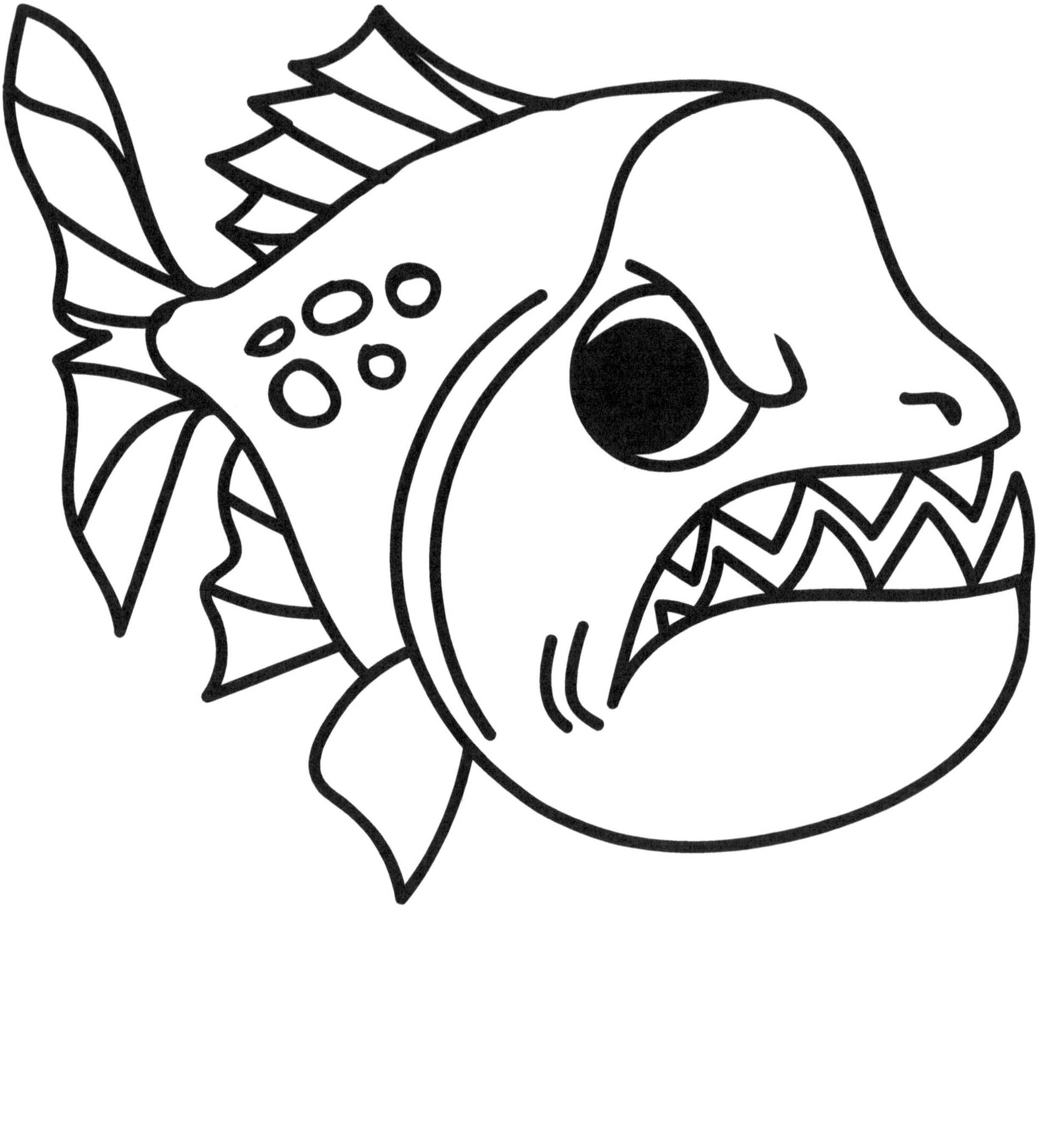

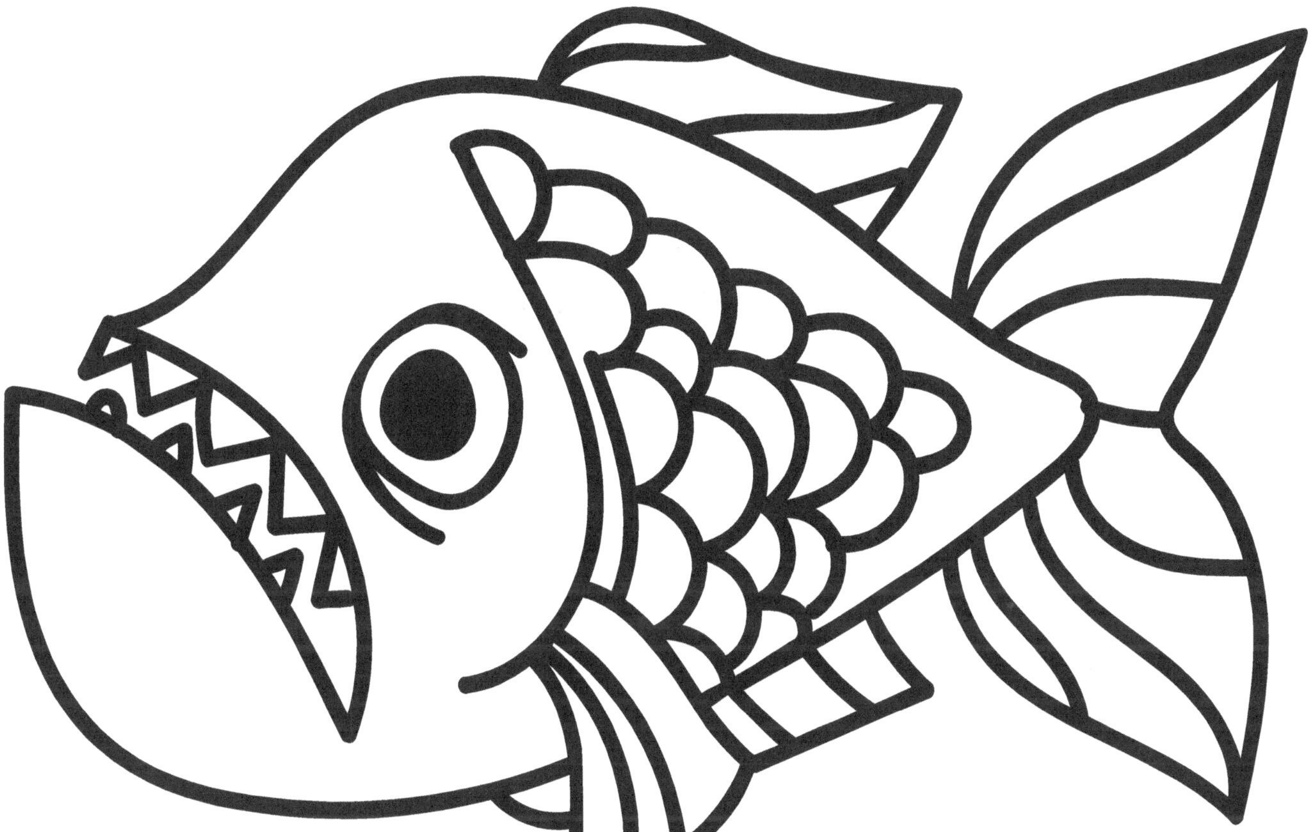

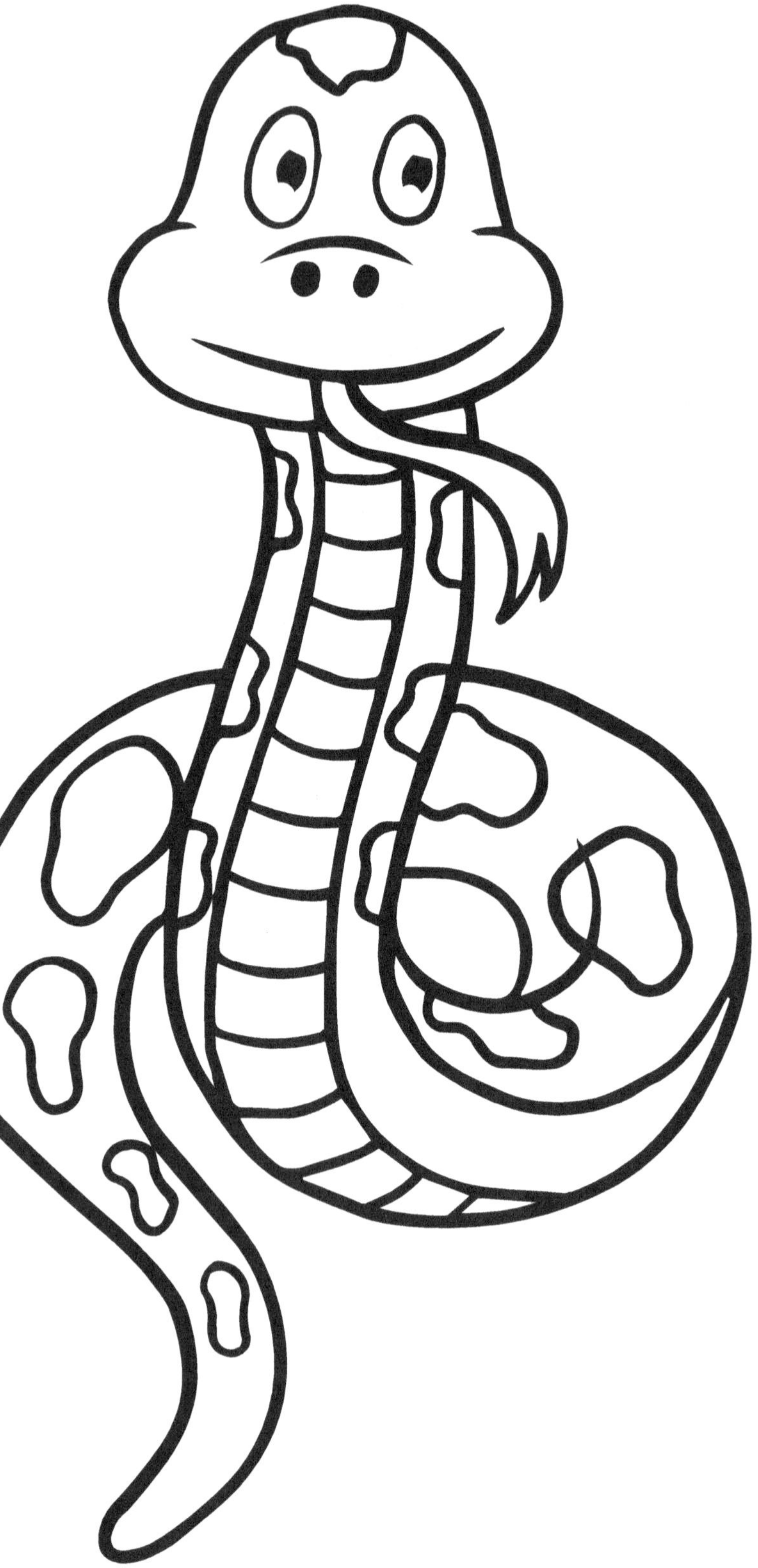

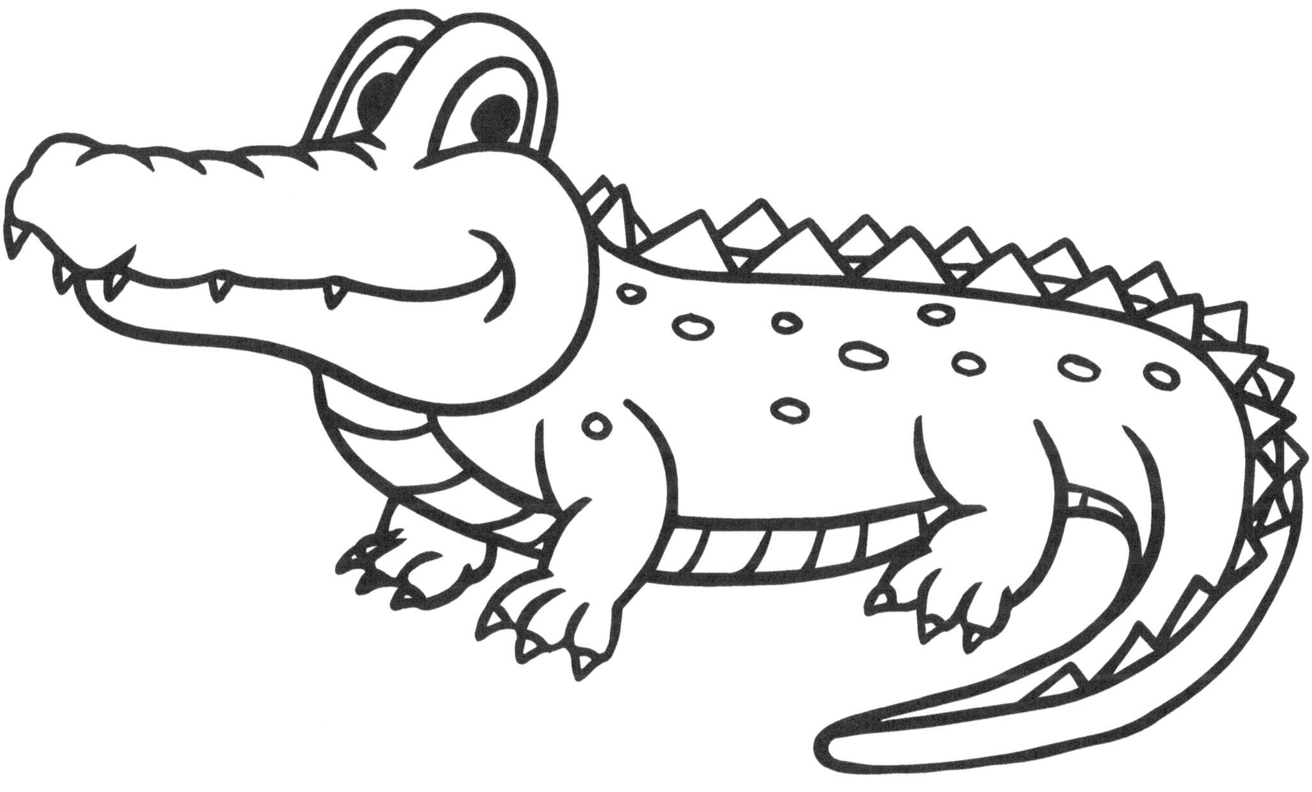

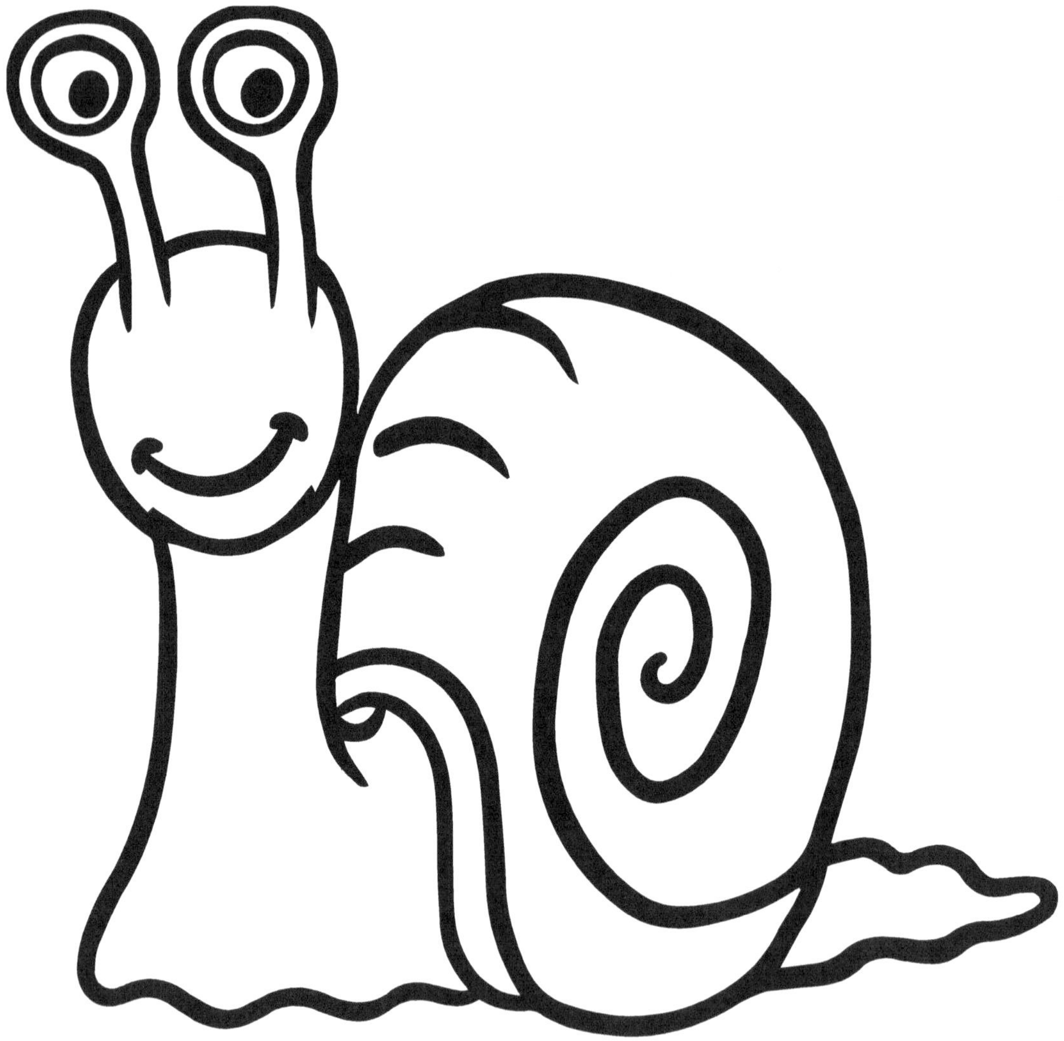

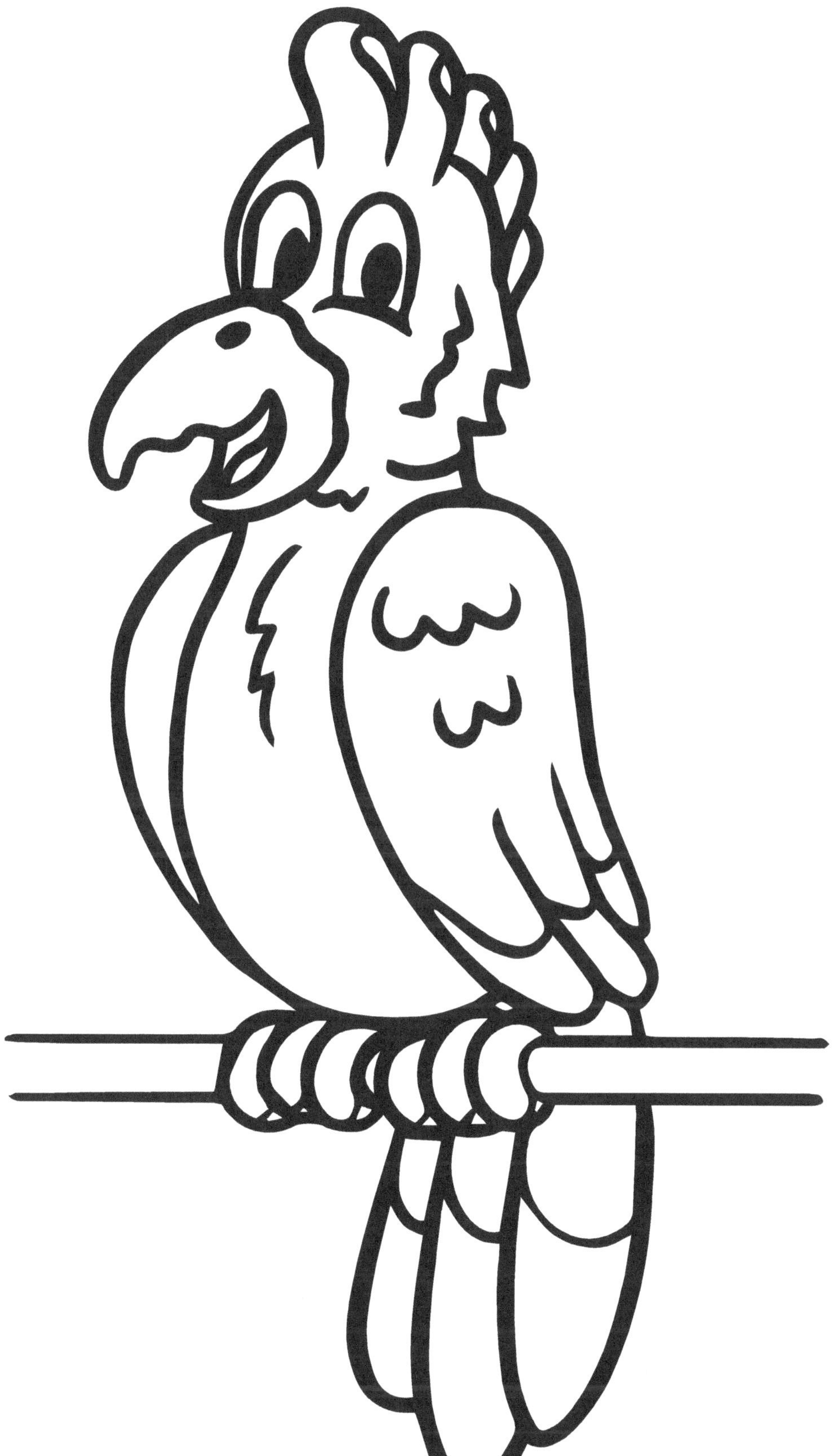

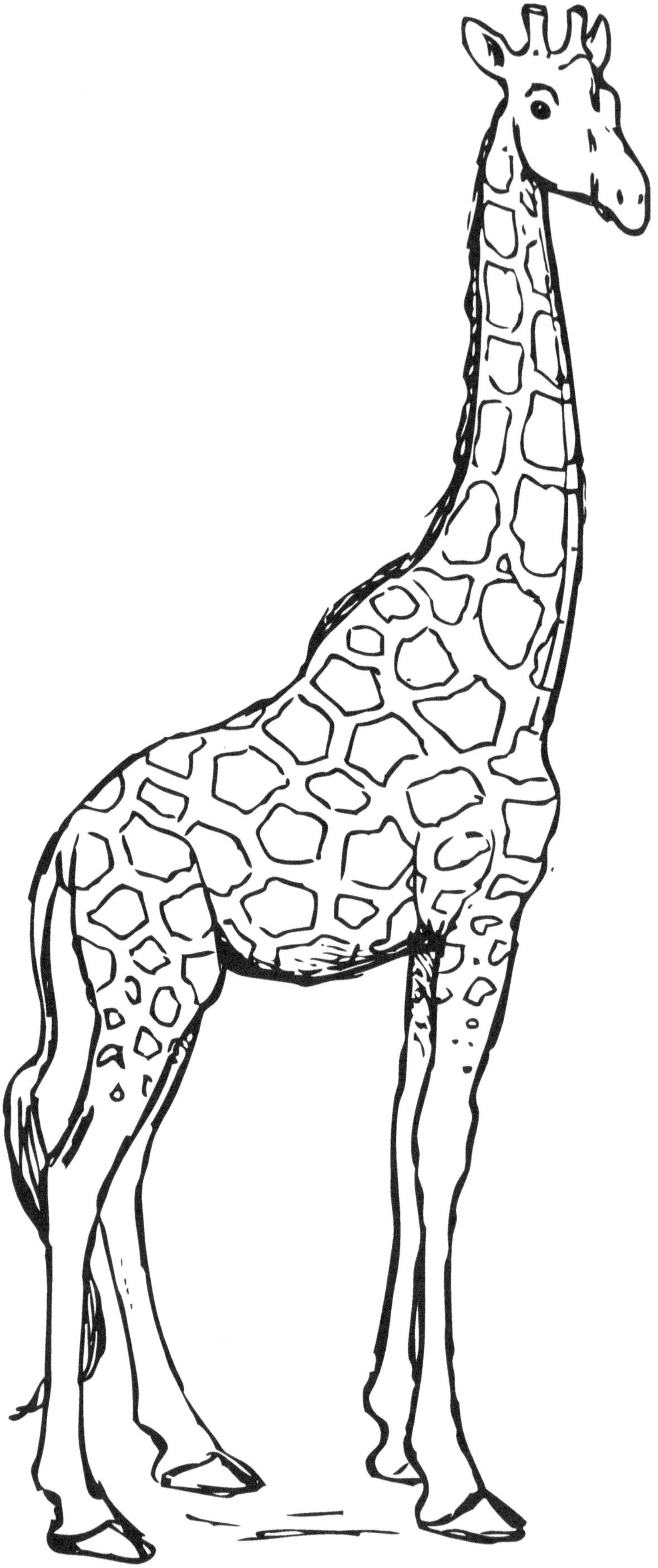

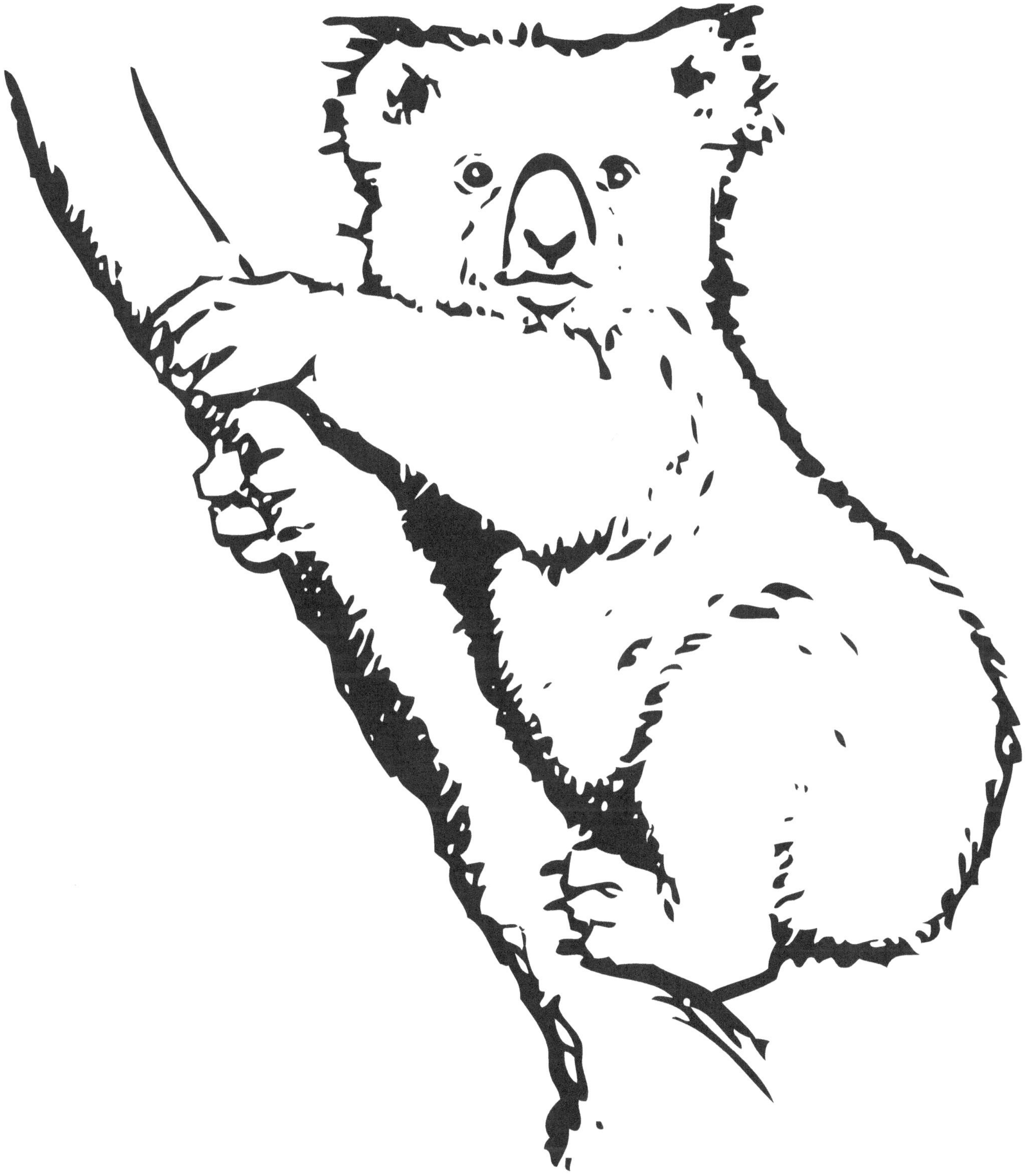

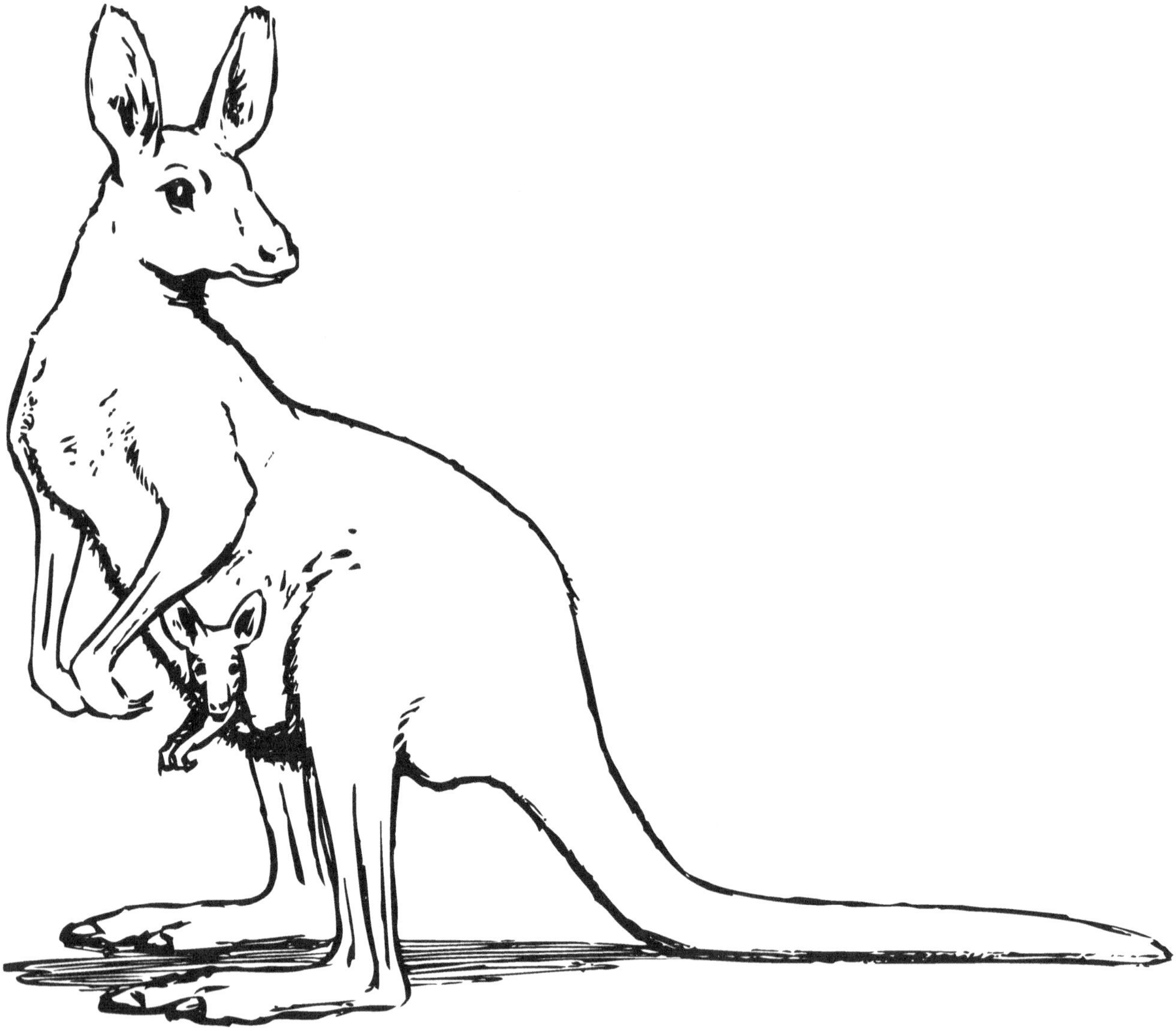

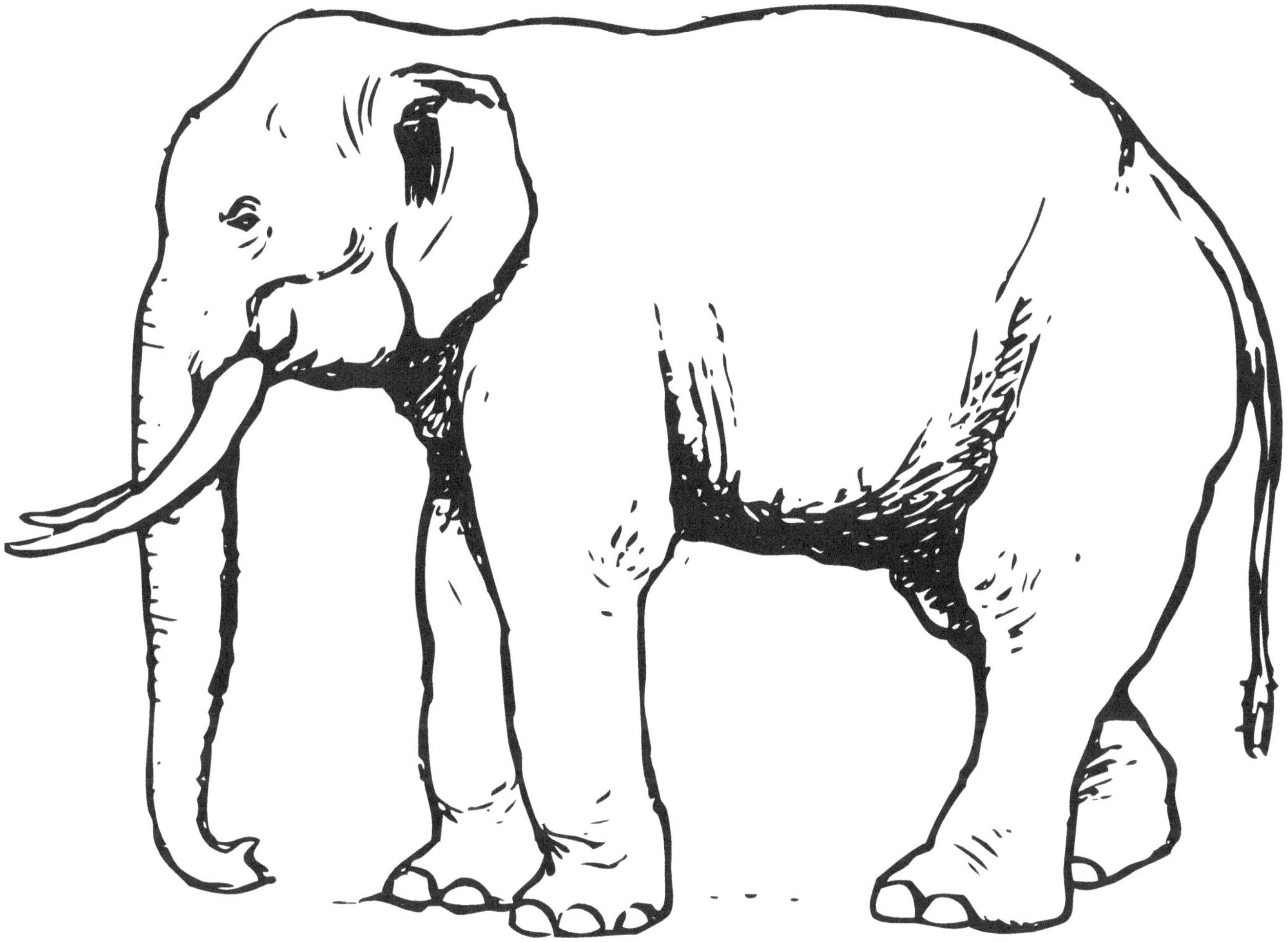

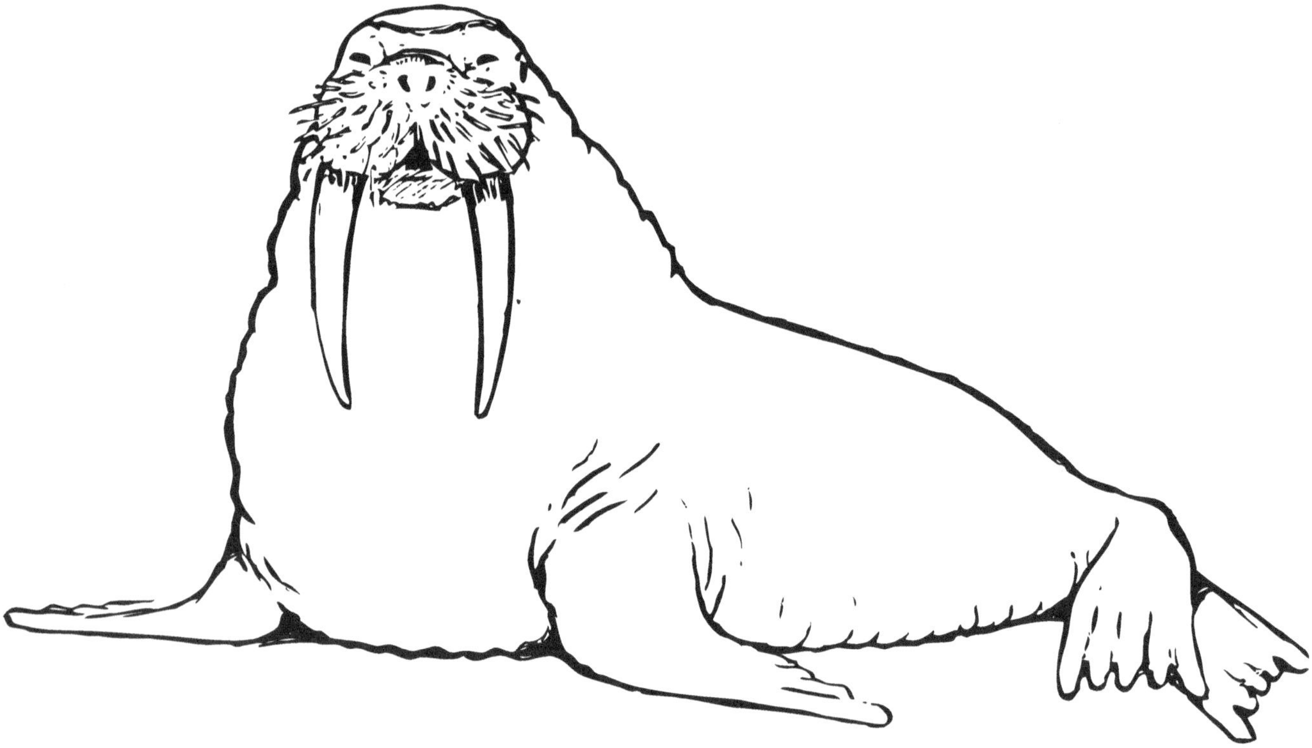

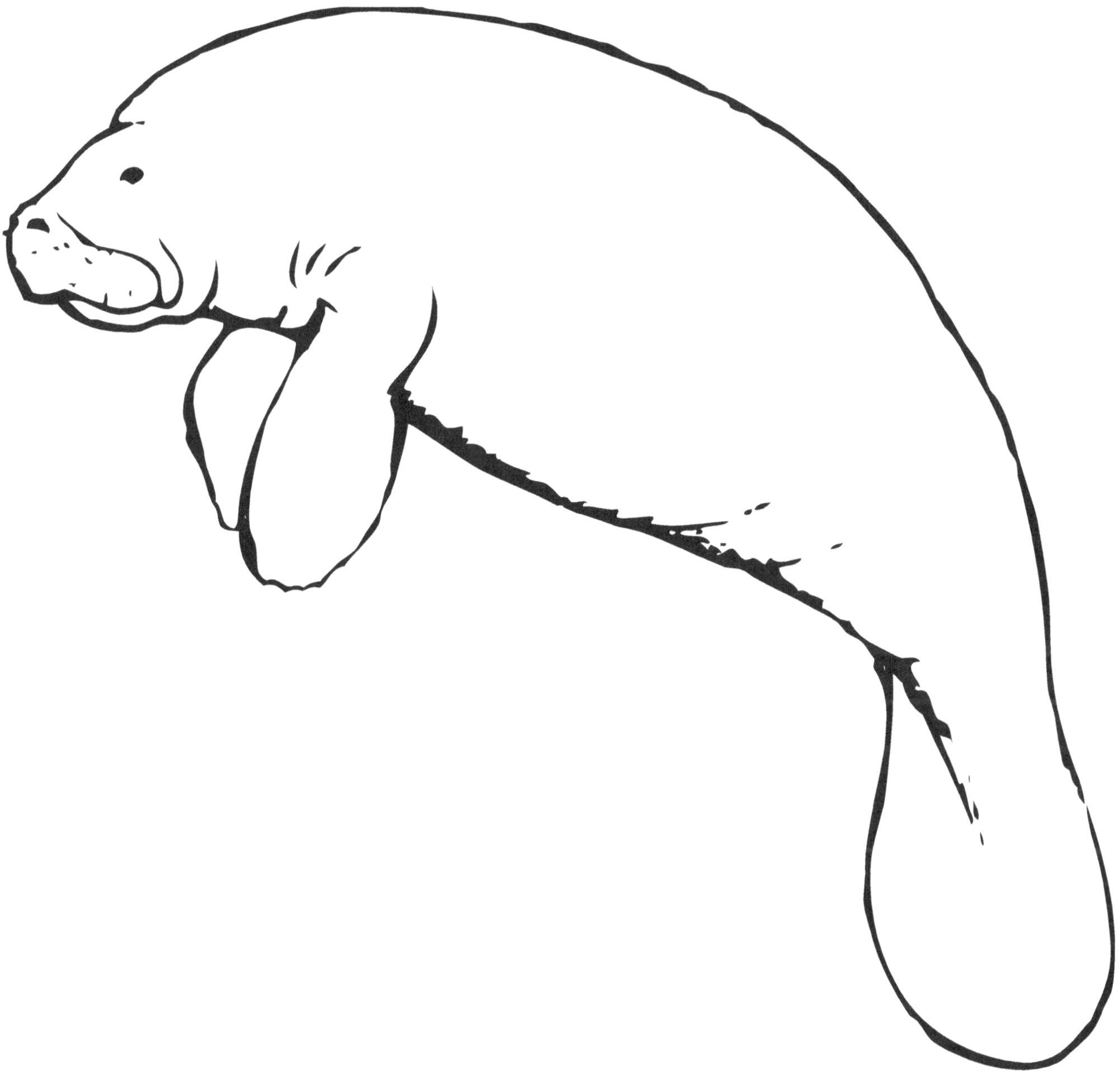

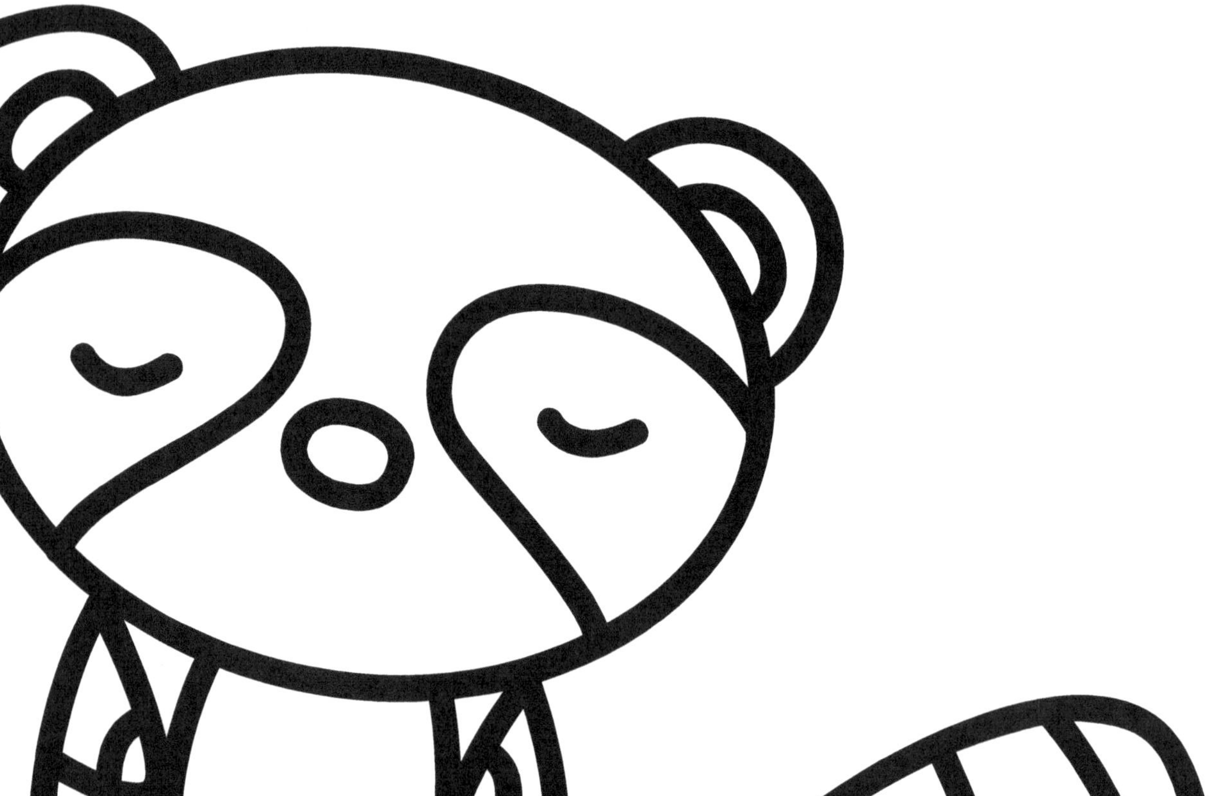

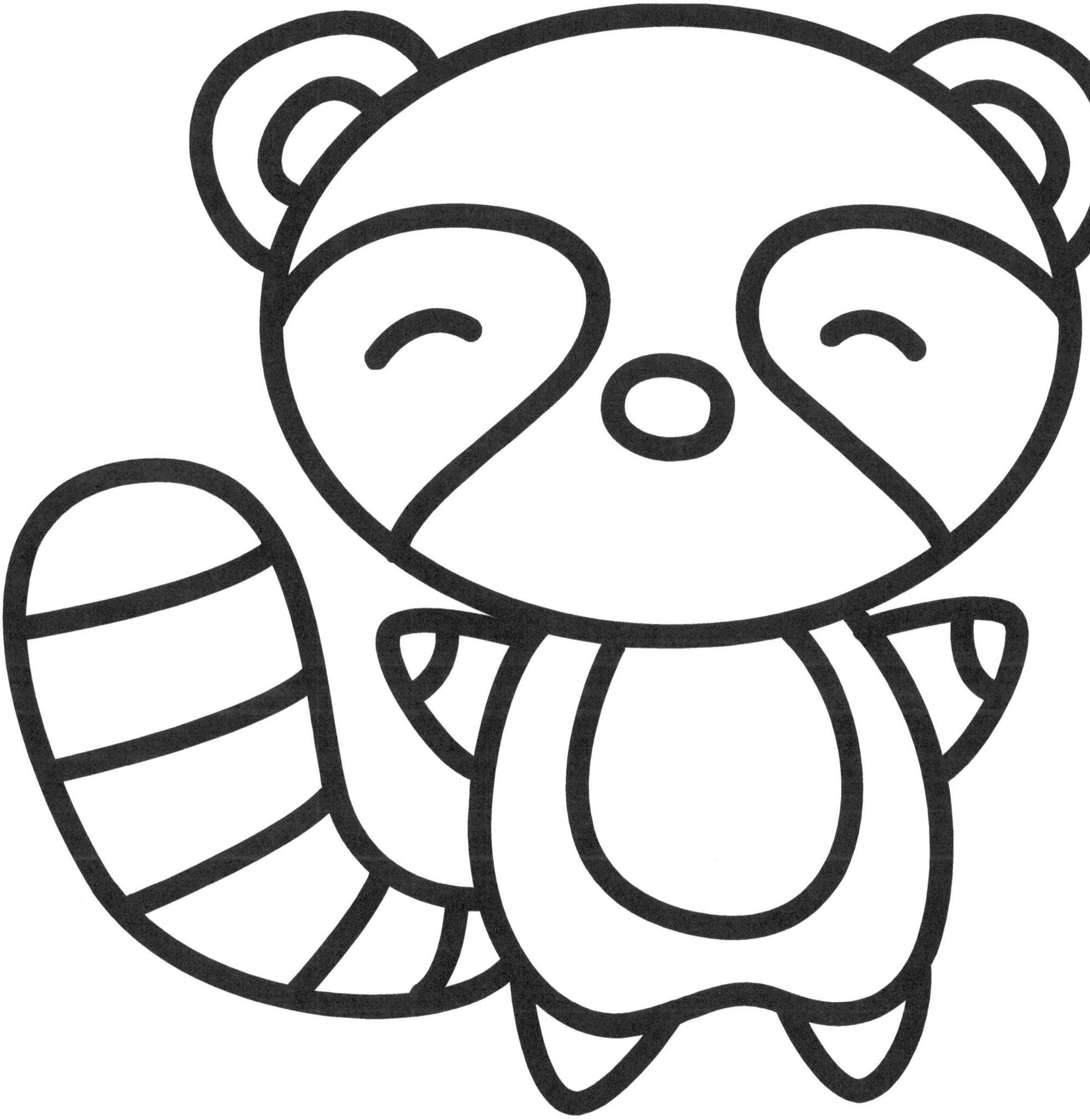

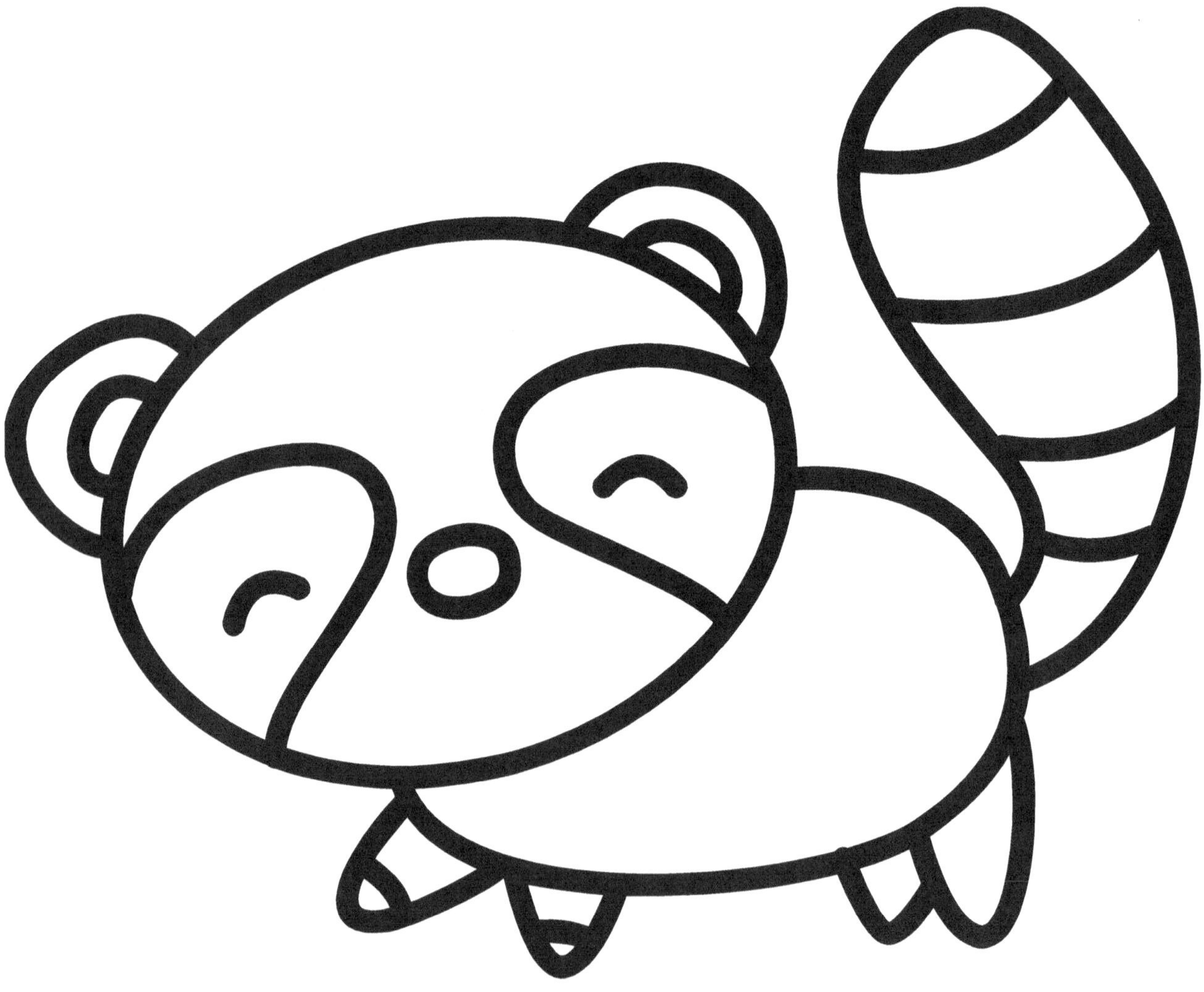

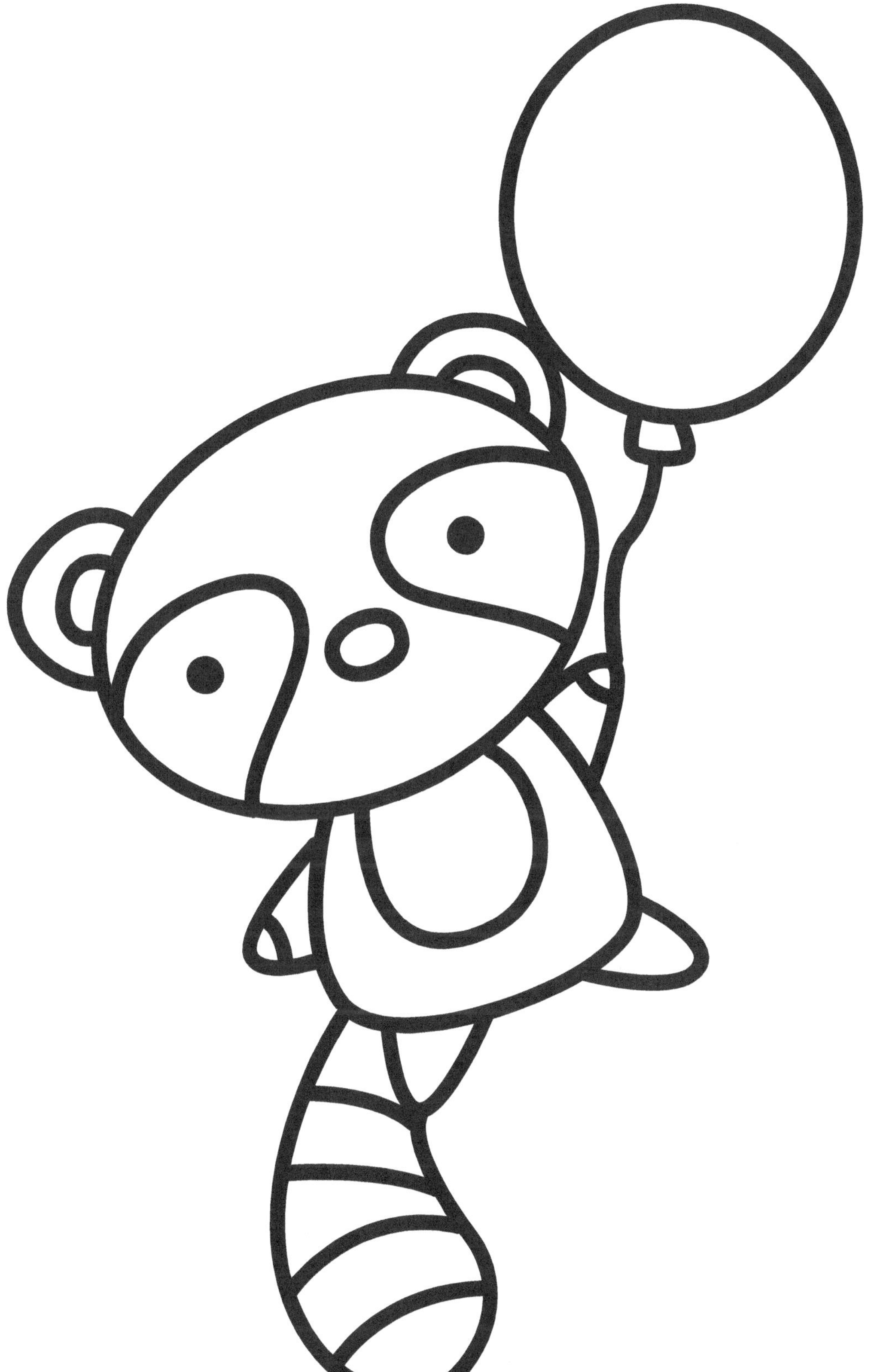

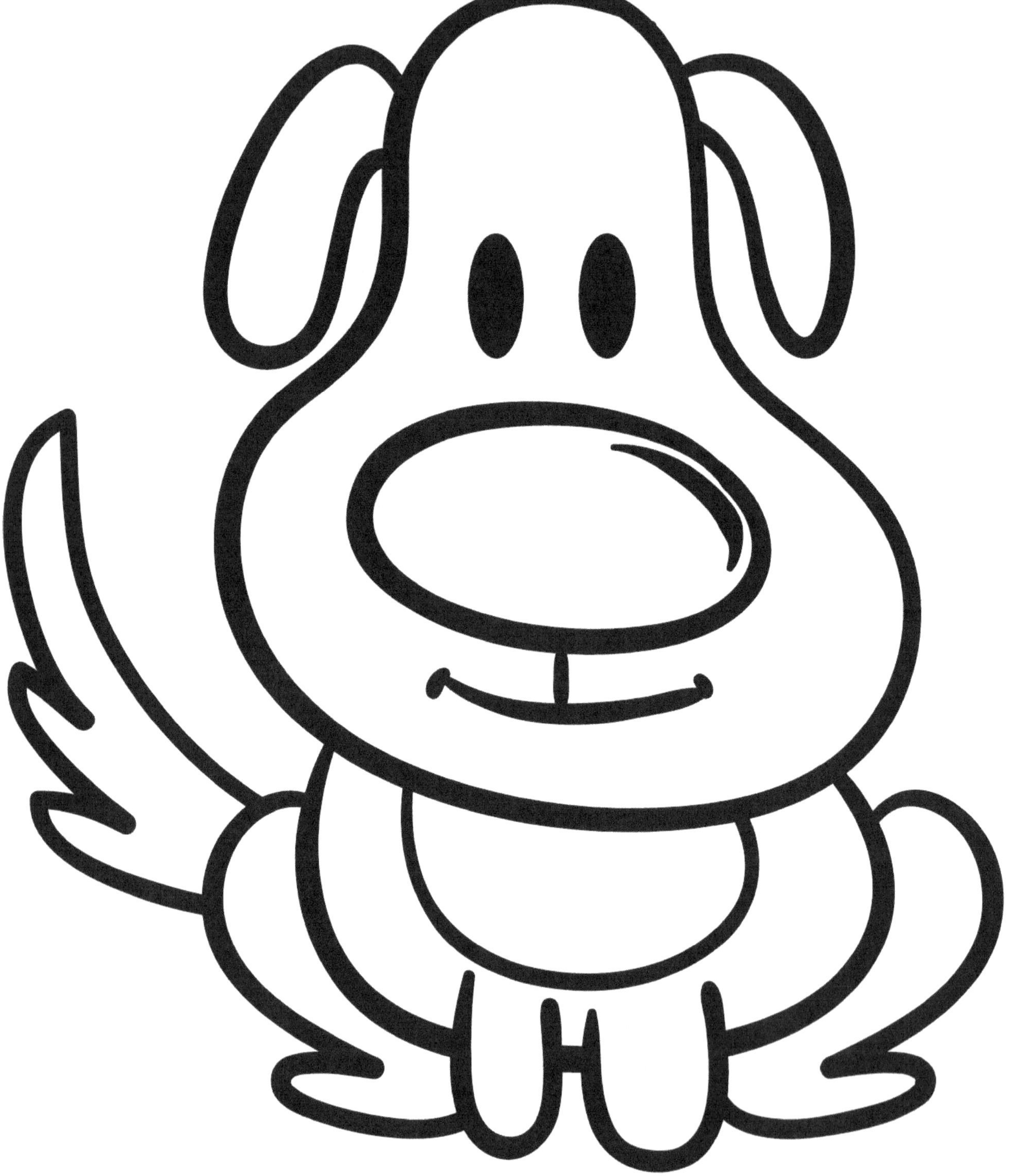

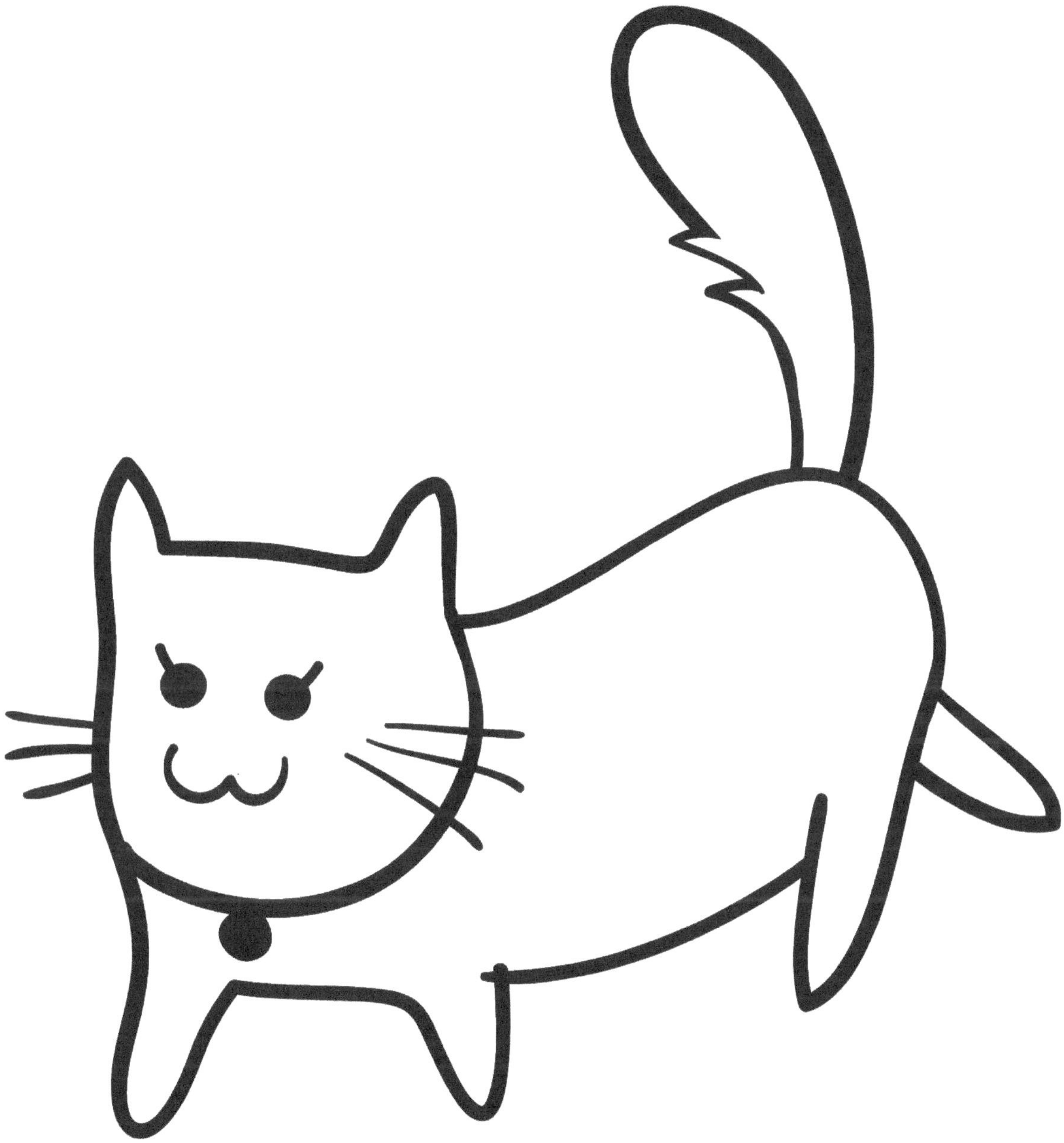

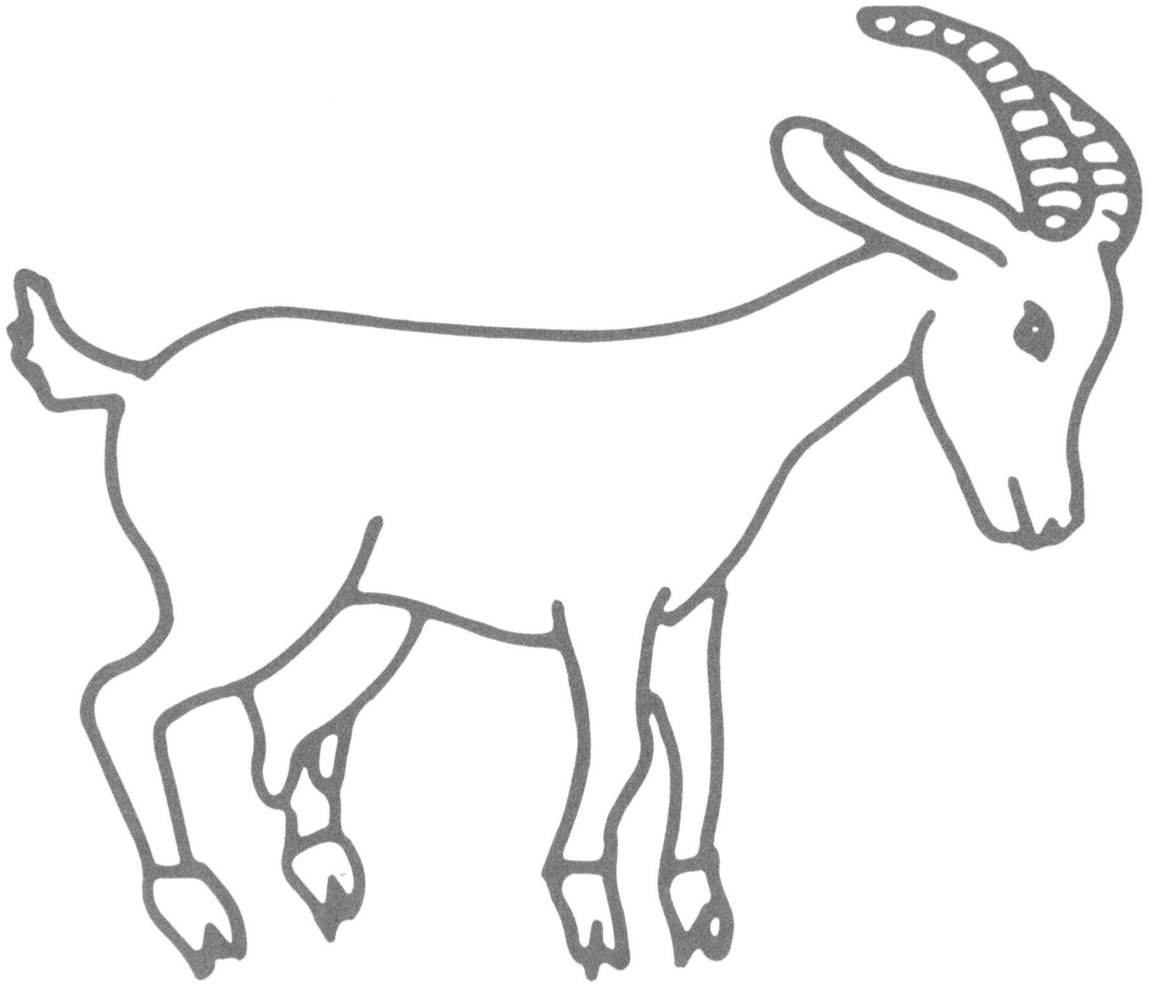

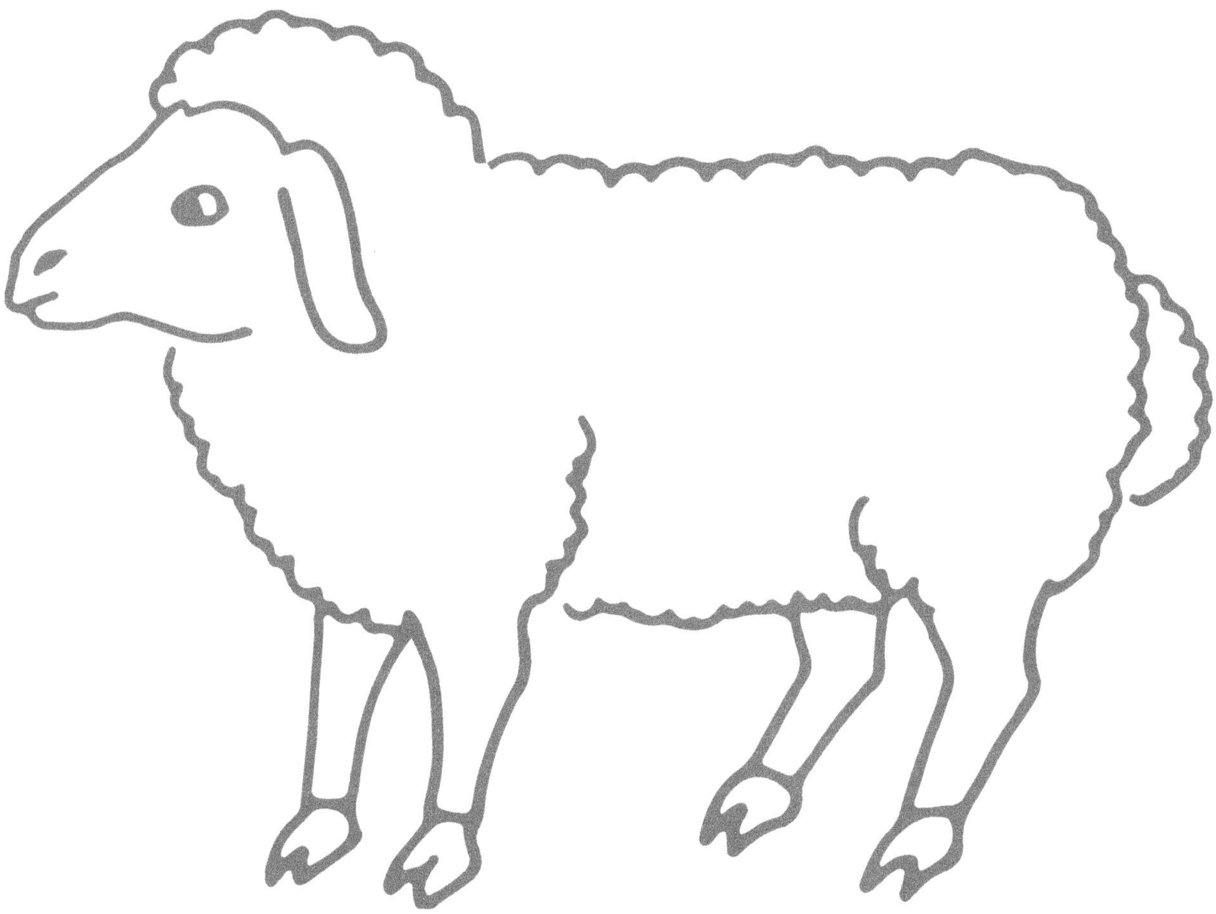

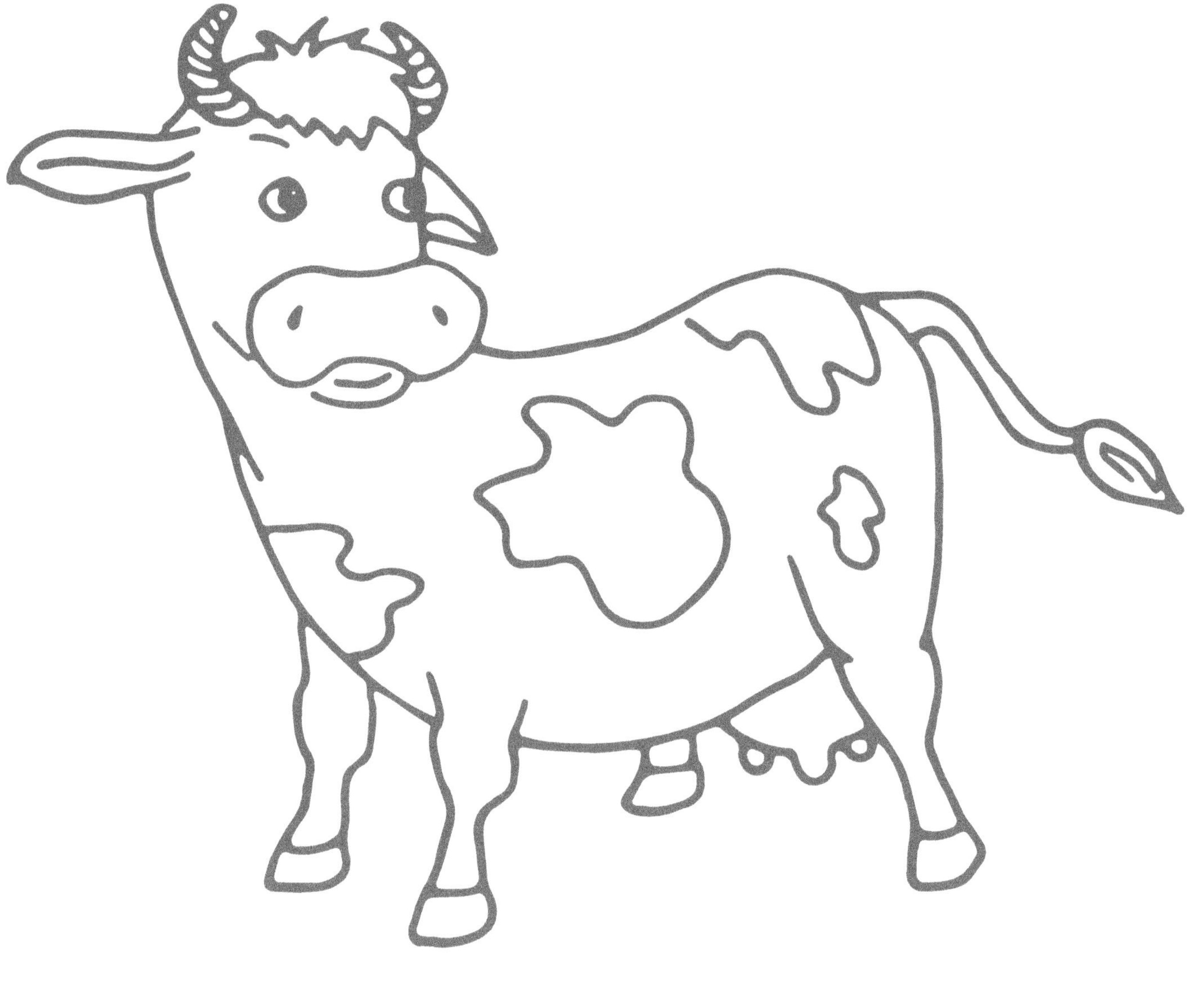

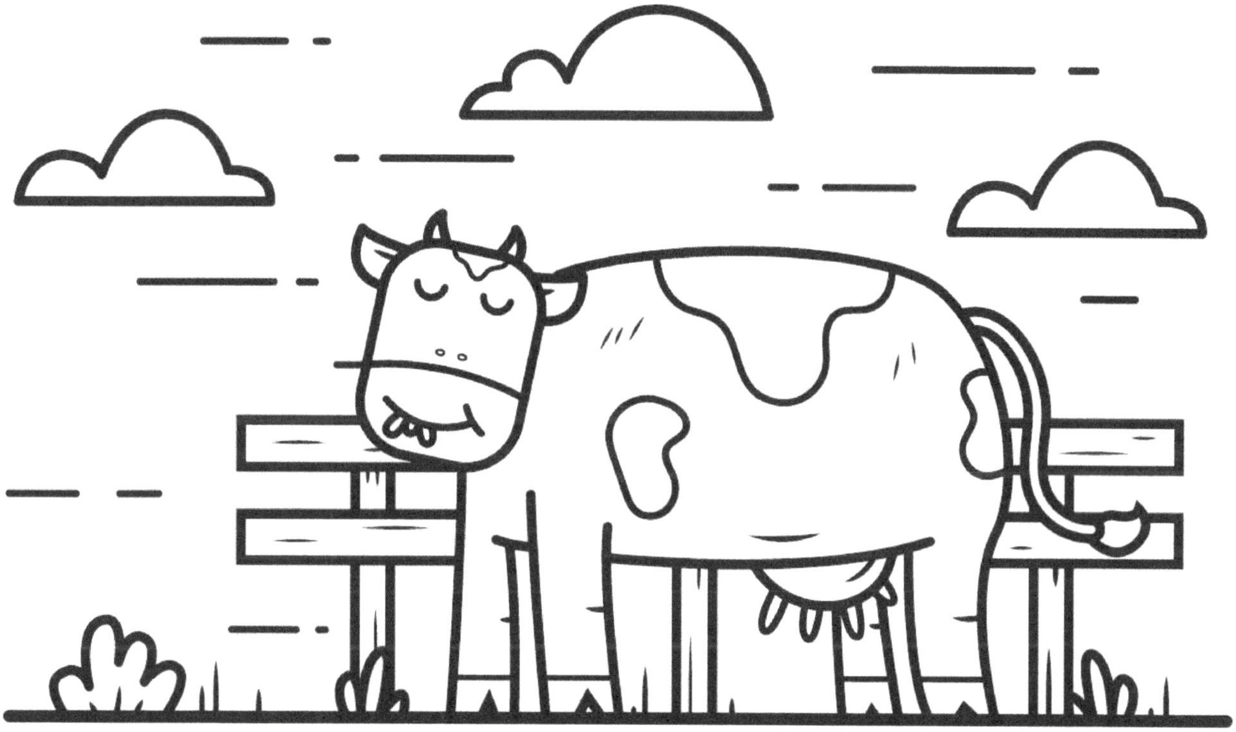

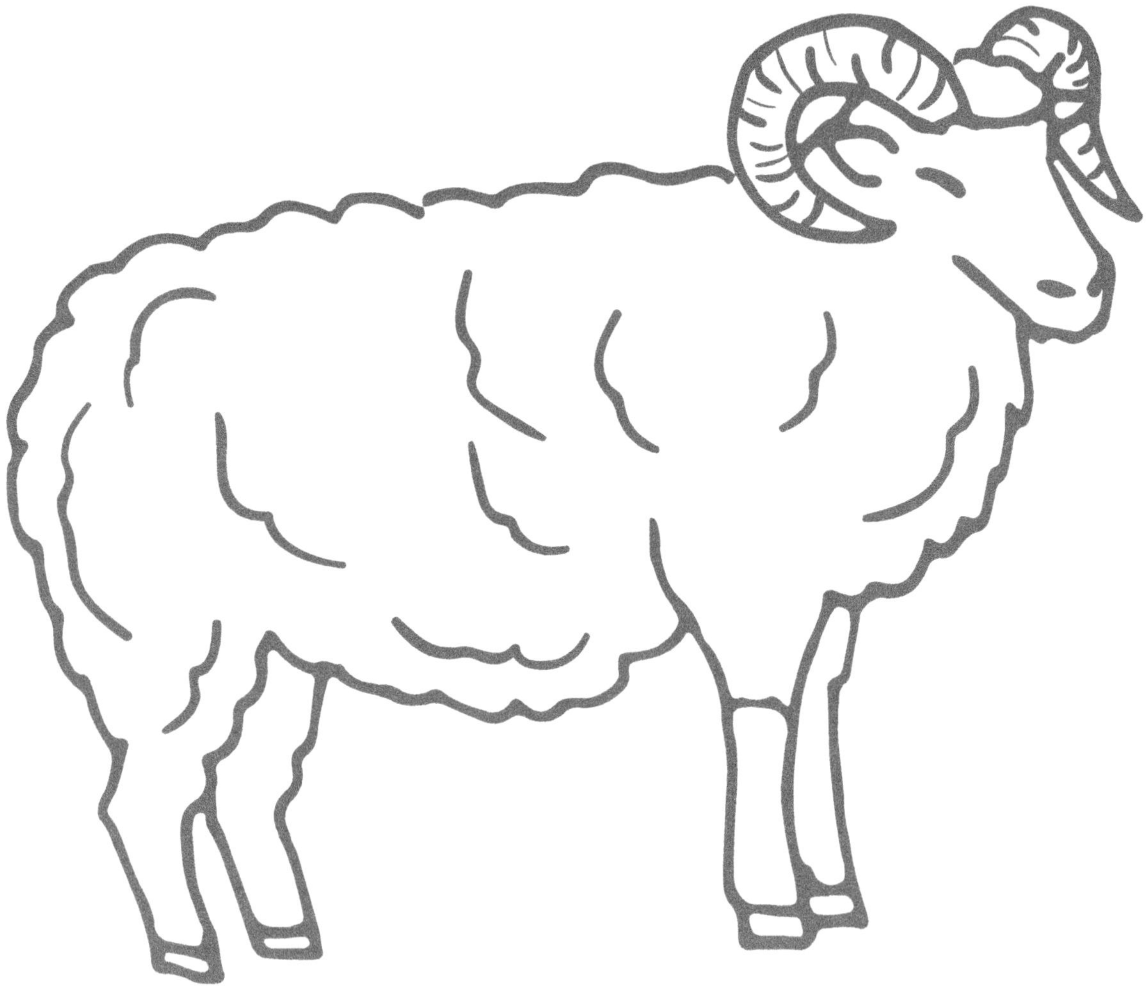

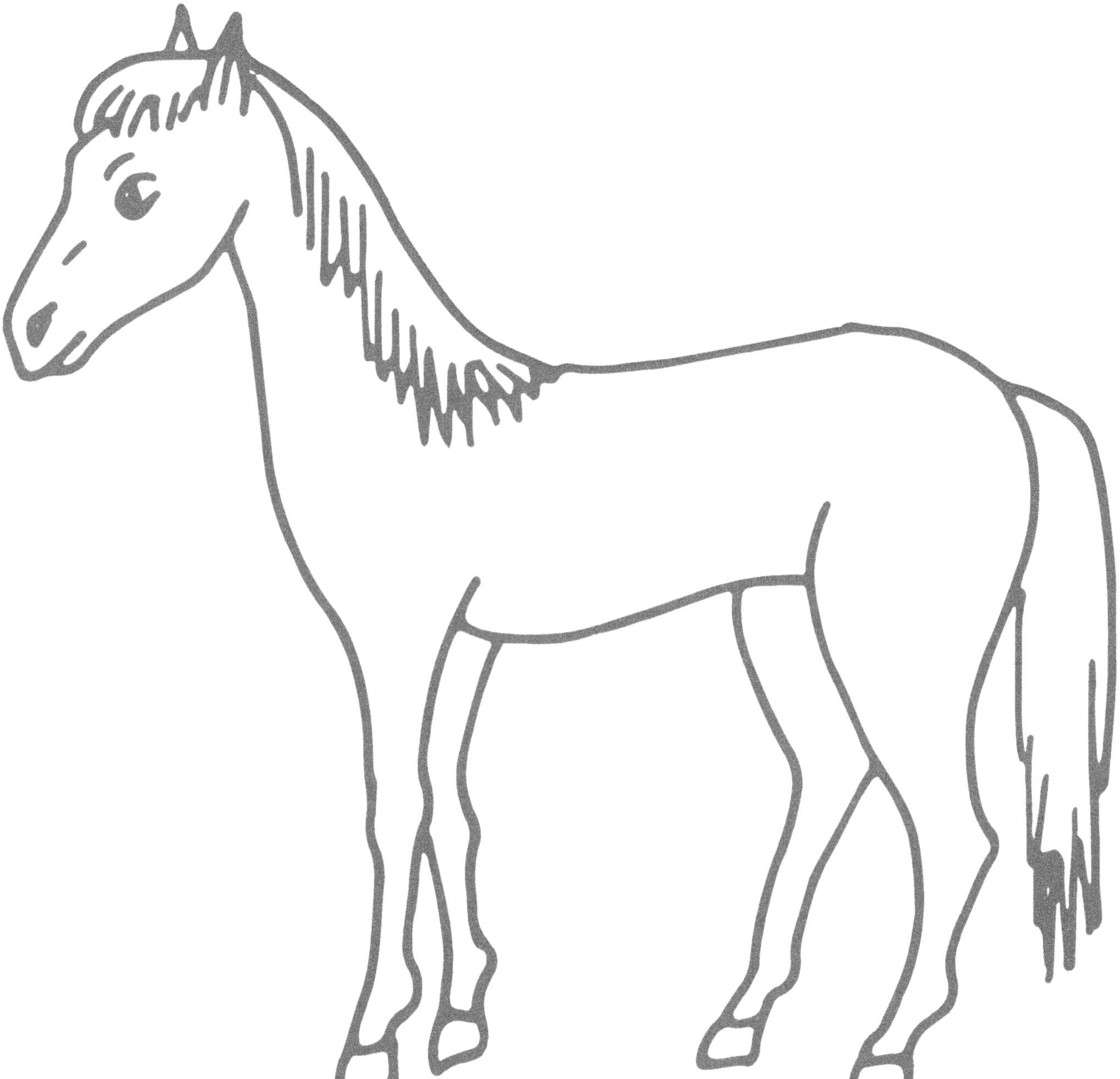

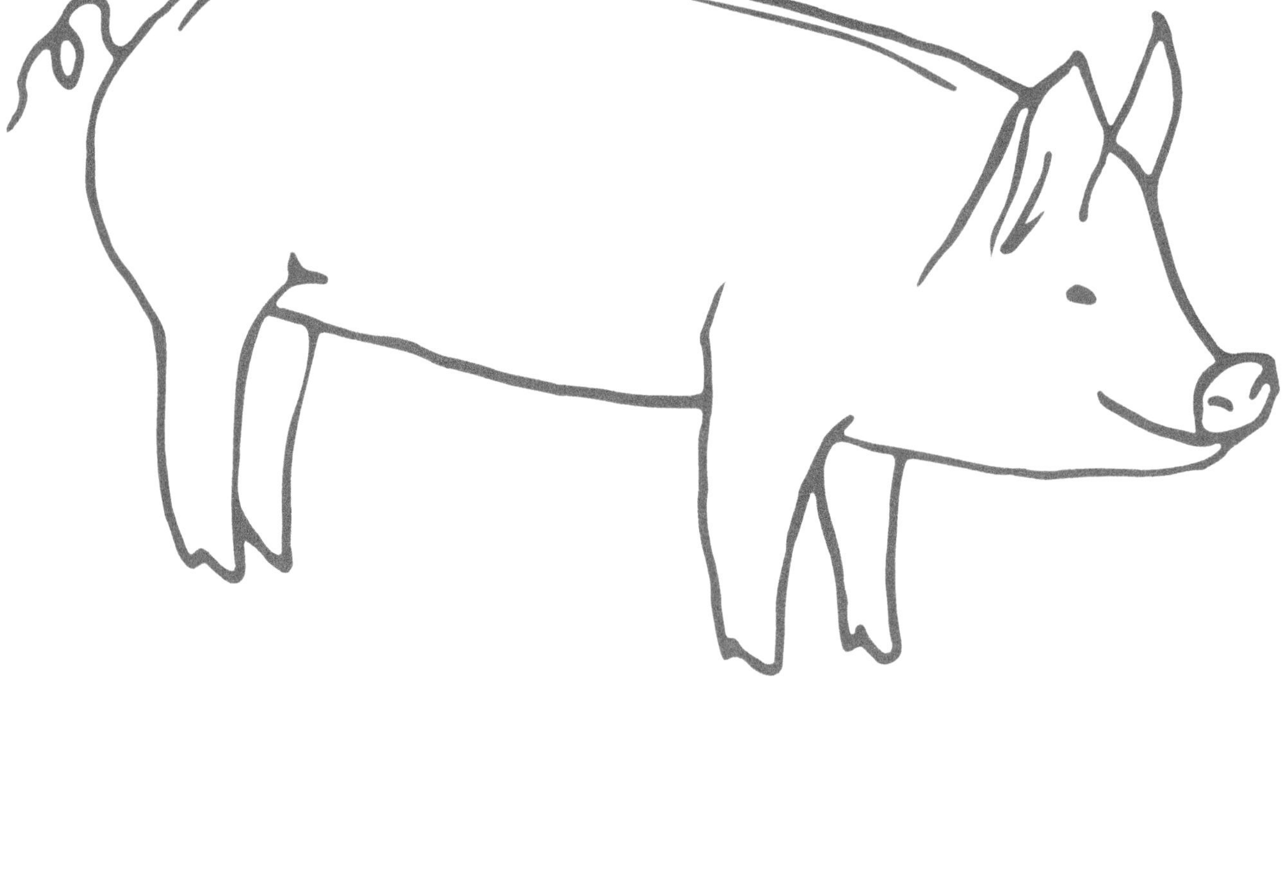

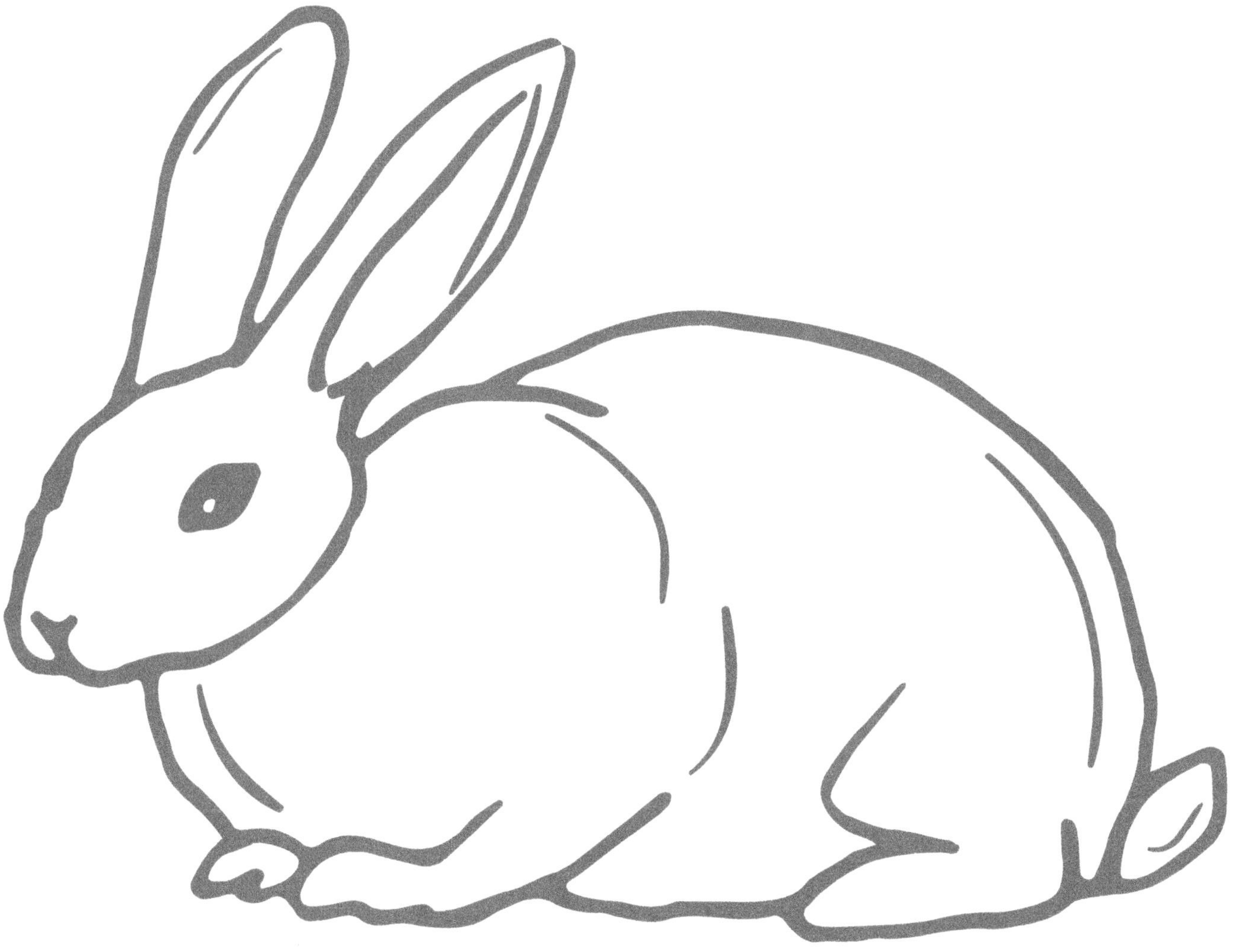

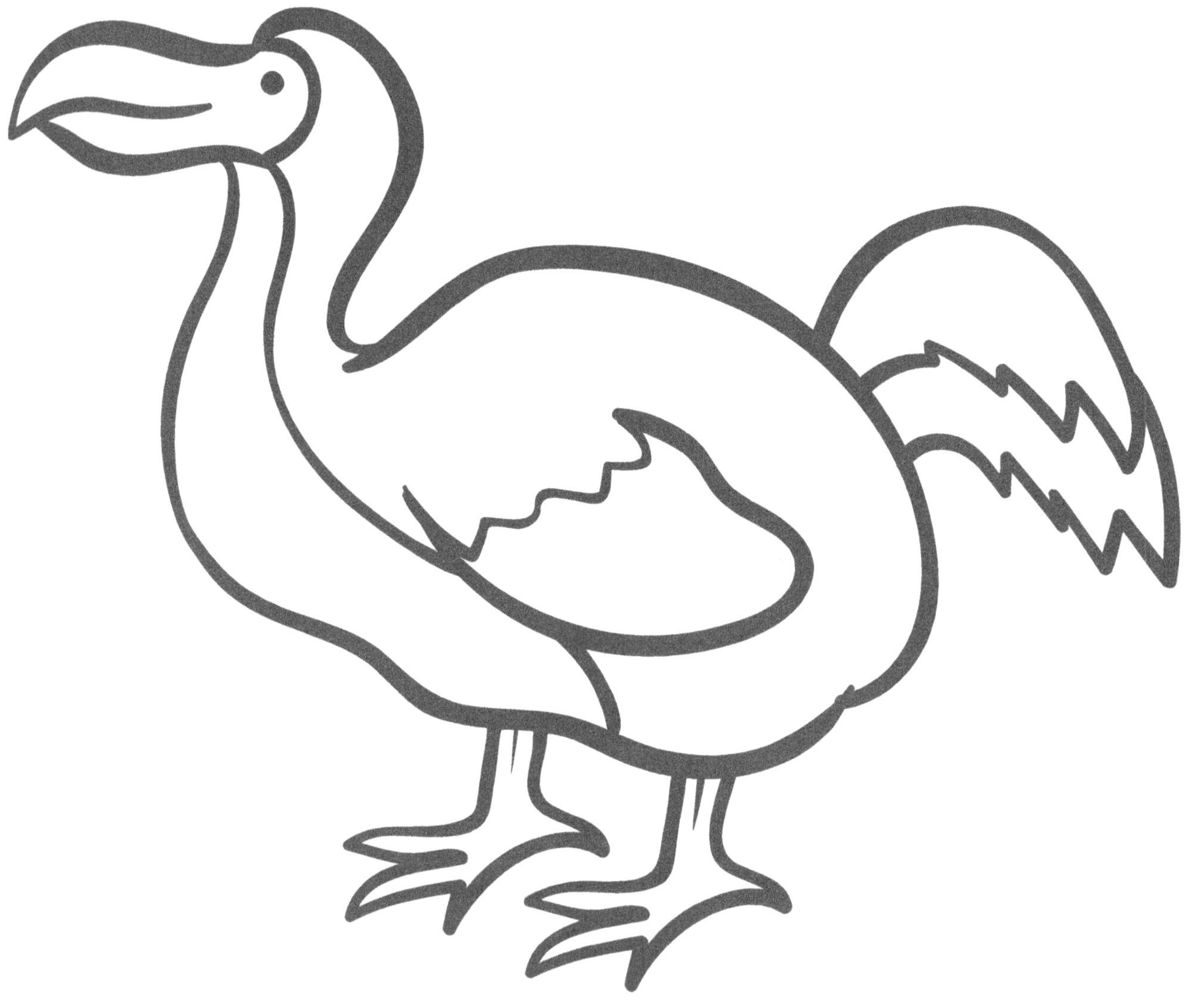

www.ingramcontent.com/pod-product-compliance
Lightning Source LLC
Chambersburg PA
CBHW081015170526
45158CB00010B/3049
9781090157942